AN ENGLISHMAN IN
THE AMERICAN
CIVIL WAR

Henry Yates Thompson in 1863, aged 24.

An Englishman in the American Civil War

THE DIARIES OF HENRY YATES THOMPSON

1863

Edited by Sir Christopher Chancellor

Preface by
DR W. M. WHITEHILL
Director and Librarian of the Boston Athenaeum

NEW YORK UNIVERSITY PRESS
NEW YORK

Made and printed in Great Britain by
William Clowes & Sons, Limited
London, Beccles and Colchester

To my Mother,
Henry Yates Thompson's niece,
on her ninetieth birthday

Some Acknowledgements

THE work of editing the diaries of my great-uncle, Henry Yates Thompson, of providing the footnotes and other editorial contributions, involved much general reading about the Civil War and the checking and verification of facts. But this work lays no claim to serious scholarship and it would be pointless, and a little pretentious, to append a bibliography. My reading has been discursive and limited for the most part to secondary sources. The source material available to students of the Civil War seems almost limitless and the number of books written about it astronomical. Nevertheless, I have some debts to acknowledge.

Some of the books that I have drawn upon are mentioned in my text and footnotes, but I must refer particularly to the works of Mr. Bruce Catton. The stupendous bibliographies attached to his books testify to the depth of knowledge underlying them; but they make lively reading and they have certainly given me a vivid picture of the Civil War. I found especially useful the trilogy, *The Centennial History of the Civil War* (three volumes, 1961, 1963, and 1965) and the most recent book, *Grant Takes Command* (1968).

I have leaned heavily on *The Cambridge Modern History*. In the 1903 edition, Volume VII, the Civil War chapters are written with elegance and distinction by John George Nicolay, who was Lincoln's secretary from the day of the presidential nomination to the tragic end in April 1865. He produced, in collaboration with his eminent friend, John Hay, the great ten-volume Lincoln Biography.

Many Civil War generals on both sides published their reminiscences, a custom continuing into our own day. Such records are not invariably good reading; but the *Personal Memoirs of General Grant*, completed just before his death, are in a class of their own and they leave an unforgettable impression of that simple, gallant and capable man.

[vii]

In the diaries my great-uncle refers to some of the books that he was reading as he travelled – among them two great books, de Tocqueville's *Democracy in America* and F. L. Olmsted's *The Cotton Kingdom.*

I have quoted several passages from Trollope's *North America* (1862). He went to America a year ahead of my great uncle and covered much of the same ground. His comments and judgements are for the most part balanced and sensible; and the book is well worth reading, although it is repetitious and could better have been half its length.

I have benefited from the advice of two American scholars – Professor John A. Munroe, head of the Department of History at the University of Delaware, and Dr. Walter Muir Whitehill, Director and Librarian of The Boston Athenaeum. Without the encouragement of these two learned friends, I am not sure whether I would have persevered; and now Dr. Whitehill, to my great delight, has set his seal upon the book by writing the Preface to it.

I am indebted also to Dr. Stephen T. Riley, Director of the Massachusetts Historical Society, who has been good enough to identify some of the persons mentioned in the diaries. He has also with great kindness helped me with the illustrations.

I must remind my friend, Mr. Robert R. Edgar, who is in charge of the forests belonging to the Bowater Paper Corporation in Tennessee, of the wet day that we spent together in February 1969 touring the sodden fields and woods of Chickamauga and peering through the mists from the summit of Lookout Mountain to catch a few glimpses of the winding Tennessee River and to identify as best we could the landmarks described in my great uncle's account of the Battle of Chattanooga.

Finally, I would like to thank Mr. William Armstrong and Mr. W. D. Procter of Sidgwick and Jackson for their advice and assistance in the editorial preparation of the book; and Mrs. K. Green, my secretary for many years, for all the help she has given me.

CHRISTOPHER CHANCELLOR

Editor's Note

An asterisk (*) following the first mention of a name denotes that the person is included in the list of biographical notes at the end of the text.

[viii]

Contents

List of Plates

Maps

[x]

List of illustrations in text

Preface

by W. M. WHITEHILL, *Director and Librarian, Boston Athenaeum*

THE name of Henry Yates Thompson (1838–1928) was familiar to me as a Harvard undergraduate in the twenties because of the respect in which he was held as a collector of medieval manuscripts. George Parker Winship, my mentor in the Widener Library, and Professor A. Kingsley Porter, often mentioned superb examples that Yates Thompson had owned, and pointed out that he was a collector so discriminating that he severely limited the number of his manuscripts to one hundred. Whenever tempted by a new one, he had to make sure that it was of finer quality than the one he already had, for its purchase would mean the relinquishment of something he already owned. Most collectors delight in crowding their shelves; Yates Thompson consistently maintained his highly discriminating standard. Moreover he made his holdings available through the publication of a remarkable series of catalogues, containing descriptions by Dr. M. R. James, Sir Sidney Cockerell, Sir George Warner, and other scholars, privately printed in four volumes between 1898 and 1912. These were supplemented by seven larger volumes of *Illustrations from One Hundred Manuscripts in the Library of H. Y. Thompson*, issued between 1907 and 1918, in which the principal miniatures were admirably reproduced.

Unfortunately, I was too young ever to have seen the collection, for when Yates Thompson reached his eighties he began to dispose of his treasures. On his eightieth birthday in 1918 he gave the British Museum the magnificent English early fourteenth-century Psalter of the Norfolk family of St. Omer (no. 58 in his hundred, now Add. MSS. 39810). He then sold a section of his collection at Sotheby's in 1919, 1920, and 1921. At these the British Museum purchased the English late twelfth-century 'Life and Miracles of St. Cuthbert' (no. 84, now Add. MSS 39943) and 'La Sainte Abbaye', written in France about 1300 (no. 40, now Add. MSS. 39843), which completed 'La Somme le

Roy' (Add. MSS. 28162), acquired earlier from another source. In 1929, the year after her husband's death, Mrs. Yates Thompson in his memory gave the British Museum no. 37 of his collection, the second volume of a French thirteenth-century manuscript Bible, the first of which (as Harley MS. 616) had been in the Museum since its founding in 1753.

On his death in 1928 Yates Thompson left the residue of his collection to his widow. Mrs. Yates Thompson died in 1941 and she bequeathed these forty-six splendid manuscripts to the British Museum where they are kept, a lasting memorial to him, as a special and separate exhibit.

Henry Yates Thompson's gifts were not confined to the British Museum. He gave another of his great manuscripts, the Metz Pontifical, to the Fitzwilliam Museum, as well as providing an art school for Harrow, a library for Newnham College, Cambridge, and three additional rooms at the Dulwich Picture Gallery. A charming instance of his desire to re-unite scattered works of art is mentioned by E. G. Miller in the *Dictionary of National Biography, 1922–1930.*

'In 1906 he presented the second volume of the famous "Anciennetés des Juifs" of Josephus, illuminated by Jean Fouquet, to King Edward VII, in order that it might be presented to the French nation for preservation with the first volume in the Bibliothèque Nationale, after the insertion of ten of its missing miniatures which had been discovered in the Royal Library at Windsor Castle; for this action he received the legion of honour from the French government.'

Having admired Henry Yates Thompson as a collector for a good forty-five years without knowing anything of him as a person, it was a delightful surprise to me in the summer of 1970 to learn that he had visited the United States for six months in 1863 and had kept a detailed journal of his travels, that had remained undisturbed in the possession of his heirs for more than a century. His great-nephew, Sir Christopher Chancellor, who had turned it up and was editing it, sent me his transcription at the suggestion of our mutual friend, Professor John A. Munroe of the University of Delaware. I was immediately fascinated with the journal, not only because of my earlier and very different enthusiasm for its author, but because of the glimpses of Boston that it provided.

When he came to the United States, Henry Yates Thompson was twenty-four years old. He had been educated at Harrow and at Trinity College, Cambridge, where he had won the Porson prize for Greek verse. Also at Cambridge he had known William Everett, son of the versatile and omnipresent Edward

Everett who had been successively a Unitarian clergyman, Professor of Greek Literature at Harvard, editor of the *North American Review*, Congressman, Governor of Massachusetts, Minister to the Court of St. James's, President of Harvard, Secretary of State, and United States Senator. Consequently, when Yates Thompson arrived in Boston in July 1863 he stayed with the Everetts in Summer Street; as a friend of the family all doors were open to him. He attended Harvard Commencement on the 17th, walking in the procession from the library to the First Parish Church beside his host, who, as a member of the class of 1811 and a former President of the University, enjoyed eminent seniority. He sat at the front in the company of two other former presidents, James Walker and the ninety-two-year-old Josiah Quincy, but after the ceremonies Nathan Appleton, one of the graduating seniors, provided a lighter interlude by taking him to the Porcellian Club 'where books and bottles filled the room'. At the Commencement dinner in University Hall Yates Thompson sat next to President Hill, listened to various speeches, and even made a brief one himself when his health was proposed by Edward Everett. During his stay he met Dr. Holmes and Charles Eliot Norton, called on Nathaniel Hawthorne and Ralph Waldo Emerson in Concord, and generally did everything there was to be done in Boston.

After a busy week with the Everetts, Yates Thompson took off for other visits in New Hampshire and in Canada, but was back in Boston at the beginning of September. As he hated slavery and had strong convictions in favour of the Union cause, he tried wherever possible to meet vigorous abolitionists, even though they were not always beloved of the friends with whom he stayed. On his visit to the Boston Athenaeum on September 3, he noted the marble bust of Wendell Phillips given five years earlier by the abolitionist-minded Unitarian clergyman, Samuel J. May, whom he had visited in Syracuse, New York, a few days before; two days afterward he called on Phillips in person.

From mid-September to mid-November Henry Yates Thompson ranged widely afield from New England. Besides visiting New York, Philadelphia, and Washington, he explored the border states, the Ohio and the Mississippi valleys, informing himself about the war and the conditions of slavery. The climax of his journey occurred on 24 November 1863 when, at close range, he watched General U. S. Grant at Fort Wood directing the course of the battle of Chattanooga. It was still possible for the inquiring traveller, however, unofficial, to have intimate access to the scene of military operations; through an introduction from Edward Everett's son-in-law, Commander Henry Augustus Wise, U.S.N., Yates Thompson was able to observe from the post of command a highly significant, as well as topographically dramatic, battle. He never forgot it. On December 9 he was back in New York City, where he concluded his journal.

After a final visit to Boston, he sailed for England just before Christmas, having spent six eventful months in the United States.

Many nineteenth-century British visitors to the United States found the country unsympathetic and peculiar. Not so Henry Yates Thompson. That the valuable and extensive list of introductions provided by Edward Everett and others (which in different hands might have obtained merely formal courtesies) often led to genuine friendships was owing to the young man's charm and good will. Exceptionally articulate, mature and open-minded for his twenty-four years, he was reflective and on the whole of an equable temperament. Slavery and slaveholders were the only subjects on which this diarist grew vehement. Accustomed as he had been to living comfortably in a situation of recognized prestige, it was natural enough for him to make himself agreeable in the drawing rooms of Boston and New York; what was ever so much more to his credit was his adapting himself without complaint to travel under sordid conditions made acutely worse by the miseries of war.

Yates Thompson's observations of details of ordinary life are arresting. Here is his account of some slave quarters on the eastern shore of Maryland.

'... went up the two wooden steps shown in my sketch into a room ten feet square. Open fireplace with remains of a big log in it; floor of earth, two windows, one on each side of the building – glass in neither and one with an old shirt hanging across it. To the right partition of wood with cracks in it; through the cracks saw a sort of sleeping place with crinolines lying about. Deal table with ten legs – a few mugs on it and a horn pipe with Union colours on the bowl. Two slaves came in, a one-eyed slave and another ... How did they feed, I asked? "Oh very well – corned beef and milk, coffee in harvest time, fifteen pounds of pork a month, some molasses."'

In St. Louis, Missouri, on October 29 the diarist

'found Governor Hamilton R. Gamble's office opposite the Court House, a domed Greek building in the middle of the town. I went up an office stair and at the top found a seedy soldier with a shabby dark-blue jacket and shabby light-blue trousers, a round back and a sinister aspect. To him I gave my letter of introduction and my card. I found the Governor a hale man, with flyaway white hair and Palmerston whiskers, his right arm in a black sling and a cigar between very imperfect rows of teeth. He nodded after reading the letter, asked me how long I had been in St. Louis, whether I was going to remain and settle. He said there was room for all the population of England in this country.'

[xvi]

Three weeks later at Nashville he wrote:

'I went out at about 9.30 a.m. in search of Dr. J. B. Lindsley, Chancellor of the University of Nashville. I went down to the steep river bank where quite a crowd of steamers were jostling one another, negroes lounging about, ambulance waggons with teams of mules, soldiers on foot and on horseback, steam blowing off, barrels rolling, sacks being shifted – and so on.'

The narrative quickens with the Battle of Chattanooga. Yates Thompson watched, standing on the height of Fort Wood with General Grant, General Hunter, and Quartermaster General Meigs, 'and there, sure enough, just three miles from us along the sparsely wooded face of the [Lookout] mountain, we saw a running fight with the Rebels retreating before Hooker's men.' The grandeur of the scene and the excitement of battle come through vividly as this account reaches its climax. So clear, so unpretending, and so objective is the telling, the reader feels he too is standing on a height beside the writer, watching history enacted.

At Louisville, Kentucky, Yates Thompson noted on November 15, 1863: 'If ever a nation deserved to live it is the United States of America.' This conviction stayed with him; for the remaining sixty-five years of his life, he was in frequent contact with several generations of American friends, and did his utmost to serve as an intellectual interpreter between his own country and the United States.

The Civil War Centennial, by its flood of books, celebrations, sham battles, and proliferation of false whiskers, made life in the United States in the early nineteen-sixties more than usually depressing. By the time the anniversary of General Lee's surrender had been reached, most readers were heartily sick of books about the Civil War. Yet the manuscript of Yates Thompson's diary, is a document that can command interest on its own merits. It has already served, more than forty years after its author's death, to increase the ties of personal friendship between his country and the United States that he did so much to further. During the summer of 1970 Sir Christopher Chancellor and I were in constant communication, exchanging drafts, photographs and bits of information as he proceeded with the transcription and editing. Having become friends by correspondence, we grew better acquainted that autumn in Somerset and in London. As I came to know more of Henry Yates Thompson from his great-nephew, my already great enthusiasm for the publication of his 1863 American diary increased. I felt highly honoured when Sir Christopher asked me to participate in introducing the book to British and American readers. It speaks for itself, for the editor's comments provide everything that one needs to know about the author, the diary, and the scene. I can only hope that many readers will share the pleasure that I have had as I have watched the book making its way from manuscript to type.

WALTER MUIR WHITEHILL

Boston Athenaeum
22 February 1971

AN ENGLISHMAN IN
THE AMERICAN
CIVIL WAR

Editor's Foreword

HENRY YATES THOMPSON was born in 1838, the eldest of the five sons of a prosperous Liverpool banker. He died in 1928 in his ninetieth year. He was my great-uncle on my mother's side and that is how I came to possess his papers. Between going to school in 1914 and entering Trinity College, Cambridge, in 1922, my holidays were divided between his house in Portman Square, London, and his country house in Buckinghamshire, my parents being abroad for most of that time. In these years he passed from seventy-six to eighty-four and I was a schoolboy. Nevertheless, he was a delightful and lively companion to me and his conversation unforgettable — witty, original, and erudite. He had not a trace of the recognized Victorian blemishes, not a hint of pomposity or pretentiousness or cant. When he died in 1928 *The Times* obituary notice described him as he was when I knew him. It suggested that the two most remarkable things in his long and varied life were his ownership of the *Pall Mall Gazette* '. . . at the most interesting period of its history' and the creation of his unique collection of illuminated manuscripts. But it added:

> '. . . the personality of the man was even more remarkable. First impressions of the large head, short compact build, square, broad shoulders, the direct glance . . . the sudden glint of laughter lighting up the bearded countenance, the gruff voice and the bluntness of address, soon yielded to recognition of the breadth of his interests and the richness of his experience. Further knowledge revealed a man of great strength of will, indifferent to the opinion of the multitude, at once reserved and outspoken, whimsical and generous. To his friends, and they were many, no substitute can be found for that ample, genial presence, with the sharp yet kindly glance, the open mind, keen yet humane, and the large heart.'[1]

1. From obituary notice – *The Times*, July 10, 1928.

[1]

In 1878 he married the eldest daughter of George Smith, publisher of some of the great Victorian novelists, including Trollope, Thackeray, and Charlotte Brontë. I remember the manuscript of *Jane Eyre* among the treasures at the house in Portman Square. George Smith founded the *Pall Mall Gazette* and gave it as a wedding present to his son-in-law, who promptly changed its allegiance from Conservative to Liberal. He then made the irrepressible W. T. Stead his editor and Stead transformed it into a powerful organ of political and social reform. This was sometimes embarrassing for its proprietor, especially at the time when Stead launched the newspaper upon a relentless personal campaign against Sir Charles Dilke, Yates Thompson's friend. Mr. Roy Jenkins, in his *Life of Dilke* said of Stead : 'He was an extreme egoist obsessed with a sense of his own power ; furthermore, he possessed to an unusual degree the essential ingredients of moral intolerance – he was a Puritan fascinated by sex.' My great-uncle used to warn me on no account to become a newspaper proprietor. When Stead published in the *Pall Mall Gazette* his sensational 'Maiden Tribute to Modern Babylon' he purchased a young girl to prove his point and bring about a much needed change in the law. He was prosecuted on a technical charge, convicted and sent to prison. His proprietor visited him in prison once a week and stood by him loyally. But he told me how much he disliked the public odium and social ostracism that he had to endure.

The second most significant thing in Yates Thompson's life, according to *The Times*, was the collection of illuminated manuscripts that he gradually built up with immense scholarship and expertise. 'My plan', he used to say, 'has been never to buy any additional volume unless it was decidedly superior in value and interest to one at least of my original hundred and upon its acquisition pitilessly to discard the least fascinating of the said hundred.' In this way he assembled a collection which for uniform excellence of quality has perhaps never yet been equalled. [He dispersed about half of it before his death. But forty-six volumes remained to be bequeathed to the British Museum by his widow in his memory.]

In 1865 Yates Thompson stood for South Lancashire as a Liberal parliamentary candidate with W. E. Gladstone. He failed to be elected, but Gladstone got in. He stood again twice ; but failed each time ; and he gave up trying after the Liberal Government fell in 1874. Later the Liberals offered him a peerage in return for his services to the Party ; but it would have been foreign to his character and principles to accept it. I doubt if he could in any case have been a successful politician ; his outlook was too broad and free from prejudice. He had no desire to excel and I believe he was exceptionally free from vanity. I am not sure that his convictions were often strong enough to move him to action ; and I suspect that few things in his life affected him more deeply than his experiences in America in 1863. When he was well over eighty he would talk to me about them by the hour. His enthusiasm for America, and the vision that came to him in 1863 of a great nation in the making, stayed with him all his life. *The Times* referred to his American experience as follows:

'In 1863 he made a prolonged stay in the United States during one of the sternest phases of the War of Secession, and was a witness of the Battle of Chattanooga, an experience which ever afterwards made him a strong opponent of war. From this root sprang the spreading tree of his American affiliations. He became the warm friend of each succeeding American Ambassador in London and welcomed to his house in Portman Square all Americans of any intellectual standing who found their way there — and most of them did.'[2]

He always loved the company of Americans and after 1863 he returned to America again and again right up to the time of the 1914–18 War. The first of these return visits was in 1866 when he went to see many of the friends he made in 1863. He took with him my grandfather, his young brother Rodie aged nineteen, who in 1866 kept the Diary for him and describes their visit to Washington, their impressions of President Johnson* and an occasion when they met General Grant* at dinner on April 16, 1866, at the home of Senator Sprague, former governor of Rhode Island. My grandfather wrote in his Diary that evening:

'Grant is a little man with brown hair and close cut beard and whiskers. Not a remarkable face: a very quiet expression and one of dogged determination. He was dressed rather shabbily in a long black frock coat, pants, etc. After dinner Grant talked for nearly an hour about the War. He said: "I shall be thirty-seven tomorrow." "You must be more than that", said Sumner.* "Well, I shall really be forty-four. I entered the army at twenty-one and have been in it sixteen years. The seven years I was out of it don't count.

'"Up to the affair at City Point[3] I was my own secretary. I then found the duty too great and my secretary only gave me those letters to read which were necessary." Colfax* suggested the advisability of a phonographic secretary. "No," said Grant, "I could never dictate. I only did it twice, when a second lieutenant in Mexico under one of our old fogeys of Generals. I can write fast enough but can't dictate. I wrote all the despatches

2. ibid.

3. City Point was Grant's headquarters on the James river in Virginia in the final phase of the War before the fall of Richmond.

about the Battle of Chattanooga the night after it was fought. I did the same at Vicksburg.

"'My object in war was to exhaust Lee's* army. I was obliged to sacrifice men to do it. I have been called a butcher. Well, I never spared men's lives to gain an object; but then I gained it and I knew it was the only way. If I had had Pemberton's command at Vicksburg, the Northern army should never have approached so near. He had more men than I had, but was no General. At Pittsburg Landing[4] in one peach orchard I could walk from one cut to the other on dead bodies, chiefly Rebels. They left 4,000 men on the field.

"'I never retreated during the whole War. On the whole I think Joe Johnston* a better general than Lee: but there is not much to choose. If I were asked to choose between Sherman* and Sheridan*, I don't know what I should do. Sherman is perhaps the best manager; but I know that if Sheridan were opposed to me with an army in the field he would fight till he hadn't a man left, and I should do the same. Sheridan has a habit of swearing and using strong language to his officers and men.

"'Lee was a true gentleman. I admire General Lee." He then described the surrender and how well Lee behaved, quite making an impression on him. On Grant's putting into the terms of surrender that officers might keep their sidearms and the men their horses, "Lee shed tears of gratitude". "Before Lee left Richmond" said Grant, "he had 80,000 to my 180,000. I outflanked him.

"'Thomas* is a good general, but too slow. He will never give in, but is too long about beginning. I was very nearly into Richmond at one time. If Lee had let me, the war could have ended and Sherman would have got no further than Atlanta. It was better as it was. For then we should scarcely have pierced through the Confederacy at all.

"'General Lee was no secessionist. He fought for his State, having got hold of a wrong idea. I have a great regard for him.'"

Henry Yates Thompson wrote his Diary at the age of twenty-four during his visit to North America, July to December 1863. His American journey stemmed from a friendship formed at Trinity College, Cambridge, with William Everett of Boston, Massachusetts. Yates Thompson, a classical scholar of distinction, took his Cambridge degree in 1862. William Everett, who came from Harvard to study at Cambridge, took his degree there a year later. He was the son of Edward Everett of Boston. Edward Everett was a national figure in

4. Pittsburg Landing (also known as the Battle of Shiloh) April 1862; a badly fought battle, but a Unionist victory and an important step in the campaign for control of the Mississippi.

General Ulysses S. Grant
(Photo: Brady Collection, The National Archive).

the United States — successively a member of Congress, governor of Massachusetts, Minister to London, President of Harvard, Secretary of State in the Fillmore administration, and a Senator. He was one of the leading 'orators' of his day in the classic style of American oratory. On November 19, 1863, he delivered the official oration on the field of Gettysburg at the invitation of the Pennsylvania State Government. He spoke for two hours on a windy day and was then followed by Lincoln's brief but immortal postscript.

On May 12, 1863, Yates Thompson wrote from Turin to William Everett at Cambridge:

I have an act of inconstancy to confess and a favour to beg. I find it impossible to sail [from Liverpool] on June 6. The favour I have to beg is that you send my ticket to my brother-in-law at Liverpool — Henry Bright Esq. Liverpool will find him — mentioning what you paid for it, which sum I have asked him to send to you. As to the inconstancy of my conduct, I simply beg forgiveness. My object here is to carry on my Italian studies and to hear the debates in the Chamber. I have received a tempting offer from an Italian to join in taking lodgings with him for a month. The temptation I fairly own is too great to be resisted, the Italian in question being a very nice fellow knowing everybody here and talking the purest Tuscan.

So I am at anchor here for a month and have told my brother-in-law to change my berth in the Scotia for one in the Great Eastern on June 30. What I do heartily regret is first of all missing your company on the voyage and secondly not being at home to lionize you over that nest of Southerner shipbuilders in Liverpool.

If you have occasion to stay there in passing I hope you will go to our house instead of the hotel. Either there or at my sister's they would be delighted to make your acquaintance. On the whole I recommend you to my sister's house for choice as her husband will have two bonds of amity with you, one as a Cambridge man and one as a native of Boston, he having visited that town some years ago and sworn by it ever since. He tells me that he has lately had a letter from your compatriot Hawthorne expressing 'a sense of infinite weariness' as regards the war and saying that 'the play (be it tragedy or comedy) has lasted too long.'

So Henry Yates Thompson sailed alone from Liverpool in the *Great Eastern* to visit the Everett family in Boston on the first stage of his six months' journey through North America. Before writing about him I must explain the reference to Henry Bright and Nathaniel Hawthorne. Yates Thompson, as the Diary will show, went to see Hawthorne at his home in Concord, Massachusetts, in July 1863. Henry Bright married Yates Thompson's sister, Mary, in 1861. He died in 1884, quite a well-known man of letters and a prominent citizen of Liverpool. In the Civil War he was infected by Hawthorne's political views and, to the annoyance of his brother-in-law, favoured the Southern cause.

[5]

Hawthorne was a close friend of Franklin Pierce, who was elected President of the United States in 1852. Before the election he wrote a biography of Pierce in which he said that the institution of African slavery ought to be fully protected under the Constitution of the United States. As a result of this, wrote Hawthorne, 'hundreds of friends in the North dropped off like autumn leaves'; but 'he had become a man of political importance' when Pierce was elected to the Presidency. As a reward for writing Pierce's biography he was appointed American Consul in Liverpool which was at that time the most lucrative office within the gift of the President. Hawthorne's finances were in bad shape and the appointment would enable him to repair them. He was confirmed by the Senate and in 1853 he sailed with his family for Liverpool.

A year or two earlier Henry Bright had been introduced to Hawthorne in Boston by Longfellow; and he was one of the first guests of the Hawthornes' at the home rented by them five miles up the Mersey from Liverpool. He was only twenty-three at this time; but he was related to many of the leading families in Liverpool and it was through his efforts that Hawthorne was drawn into Liverpool society and attended a number of 'elaborate dinners given by Liverpool magnates'.

On returning to America from Liverpool, Hawthorne said that he liked Bright better than any other person he had met in England. His last act as American Consul in Liverpool was to travel to Cambridge to see Bright, a graduate of Trinity College, receive an honorary M.A. degree. In 'Our Old Home', his English sketches, he calls Bright 'the best of English friends' and describes the visits of 'a young English friend, a scholar and literary amateur, between whom and myself there sprang up an affectionate regard. He talked with me about his own national characteristics and mine with such frank and admirable assertion of English prejudices that I understood his countrymen infinitely the better for him.'

As for Hawthorne, after the dedication of 'Our Old Home' to Pierce in September 1863 he became sadly discredited in Boston circles. Pierce was branded as a 'copperhead', the name given in the North to those who favoured the South, tolerated slavery and opposed the War (a copperhead being a cunning and poisonous species of snake). Exactly a fortnight before Yates Thompson visited him at Concord, Hawthorne had been so indiscreet as to sit on a platform in support of Pierce who made a speech condemning the War. Harriet Beecher Stowe*, authoress of the best-seller *Uncle Tom's Cabin*, complained that Hawthorne 'dared to patronise such a traitor to our faces: I can scarce believe it!' Emerson* in his journal referred to Hawthorne's 'perverse politics and unfortunate friendship for that paltry Franklin Pierce'. Hawthorne died in the care of his friend, Franklin Pierce, in May 1864.

When Yates Thompson arrived in Boston on July 10, 1863, the tide was

[6]

beginning to flow for the Union. Vicksburg had fallen to Grant on July 4 with the surrender of Pemberton's army of 31,000 men. Port Hudson surrendered on July 9 thus bringing the whole length of the Mississippi under Northern control. President Lincoln wrote in a famous letter : 'The signs look better. The Father of Waters again goes unvexed to the sea.'

On the same day that Vicksburg fell, Lee was stopped at Gettysburg and compelled to return south across the Potomac after suffering casualties of 36,000 killed, wounded, and missing.

More than a year and a half of bitter fighting still lay ahead ; but from now onwards the South had to fight a mainly defensive war and the vastly greater power and resources of the Union steadily bore down upon the secessionist States. The inevitability of a final Federal victory became apparent to the young observer from Liverpool. But to his friends in England and his family in Liverpool the outcome seemed still to be in the balance, and English sympathies ran strongly with the South.

In October 1862 Gladstone, Chancellor of the Exchequer in Palmerston's Government, said in an important speech in Newcastle :

'We know quite well that the people of the Northern states have not yet drunk of the cup which all the rest of the world see they nevertheless must drink of. We may have our own opinions about slavery ; we may be for or against the South ; but there is no doubt that Jefferson Davis and other leaders of the South have made an army ; they are making, it appears, a navy ; and, what is more than either, they have made a nation.'

He added : 'We may anticipate with certainty the success of the Southern states so far as regards their separation from the North.'

This speech made a great sensation. It called forth a vigorous protest from the United States Government. Charles Francis Adams, American Minister in London, wrote to William H. Seward* the Secretary of State, describing how, in an interview with the Foreign Secretary, Lord Russell, he had suggested the necessity 'to put his travelling equipage in readiness' adding that 'his Lordship took the hint and intimated as generally as possible that Lord Palmerston and other members of the Government regretted the speech'.

Russell wrote to Gladstone saying that he had 'gone beyond the latitude which all speakers must be allowed'. And John Bright* wrote to his friend, Senator Charles Sumner in Washington, saying :

I write to you from a feeling of anxiety. You will see what is being said here by public men on your question, and most of all, and worst of all, by our old friend Mr. Gladstone. He has made a vile speech at Newcastle full of insulting pity for the North and of praise and support for the South. He is unstable as water in some things. He

is for union and freedom in Italy and for disunion and bondage in America. A hand-
ful of Italians in prison in Naples without formal trial shocked his soul so much
that he wrote a pamphlet; but he has no word of sympathy for the millions of the
bondsmen of the South.

In the American Civil War, with a few notable exceptions, most articulate Englishmen were hostile to the North. On at least two occasions war became a definite possibility; and this would not have been unpopular in either country. The first occasion was when in the autumn of 1861 Mason* and Slidell, two Confederate Commissioners on their way to Europe, were removed from the British mail steamer *Trent* by an over-zealous Federal naval commander. The second was in process of being played out in the summer of 1863 when Yates Thompson was writing his Diary in America. It arose from the affair of the 'ironclad rams', two armoured vessels being built by a Mr. Laird in Liverpool. This controversy crops up more than once in the earlier parts of the Diary and requires some explanation. But it must be seen against the wider background of Anglo-American relations at that time.

I have always been disconcerted by the British attitude during the American Civil War. It seems clear enough to us today that the chief cause of the War was Northern opposition to the extension of slavery in the new States of the Union. When the Southern States finally decided to secede, the North accepted war rather than acquiesce in the dismemberment of a great and growing country. Slavery was really at the heart of the matter; and 'chattel slavery' in the second half of the nineteenth century was a repugnant anachronism. But when the War started the issue became obscured. The Federal Government, by its own declaration, was fighting only to preserve the Union and for nothing else; and emancipation of the slaves was not an acknowledged war aim. This influenced the attitude of many enlightened men in England who otherwise would have been stronger for the North. The long and complicated political struggle between North and South leading up to the War had not been followed or understood by people in England, who oversimplified the whole picture. Assuming that the 'peculiar institution' of African slavery was accepted by the North, they looked upon the secessionist States as an oppressed people fighting against intolerable and unjust Federal pressure. The difficulties and problems facing Lincoln were simply not understood. Step by step, with infinite care and patience, he edged his way towards emancipation. But in the North the abolitionists were far from being in the majority; and Lincoln did not dare in the early stages of the War to risk trouble in the border slave States that remained loyal to the Union. It was only after his much needed and expensively gained victory at Antietam in September 1862 that he felt strong enough to issue his first Emancipation

[8]

Proclamation declaring that all slaves in territory at that time in rebellion against the Union should be 'thence, thenceforward and forever free'. This was a turning point because from then onwards, in assessing the claims to sympathy of North and South, England knew that the future of African slavery was in the reckoning.

It must be confessed that, although official neutrality was now assured unless a new and grave situation arose, dislike of the North remained strong in England. Although the importance of the Emancipation Proclamation was realized it was welcomed at first grudgingly. Lord Russell saw in it 'no declaration adverse to slavery'; and said that it ought not 'to satisfy the friends of abolition who look for total and impartial freedom for the slave and not for vengeance on the slave-owner'. The *Illustrated London News* reflected the prevailing mood in turgid prose: 'That it [*the Proclamation*] will help in any material degree to retrieve the misfortune of the North we strongly doubt; that it exhibits the sentiment for the North in a light likely to do credit to themselves we are sorry to find ourselves precluded from asserting. But that it heralds the approaching doom of slavery we look upon as demonstrable.'

Unhappily a new and grave situation did arise early in 1863 and it brought a renewal of serious tension between the two countries. Liverpool was in its golden age and its ship-building industry flourished. 'Dixie Line' was the name given by the North to the ships in Liverpool's shipyards under construction for the Confederacy. This was a continuing source of provocation, and it kept poor Mr. Adams busy in London transmitting protests from Washington to the British Government.

There was no clear ruling in international law about a neutral supplying a combatant with ships, not armed but capable when delivered of quick conversion into vessels of war.

The North could build its own fleet. The South had no such facilities and gladly purchased from Liverpool fast frigates to be armed after leaving British waters. In the North this was regarded as a most unfriendly activity on the part of Britain. The *Alabama* had steamed out of Liverpool in July 1862: it was taken over and armed as a Confederate raider in the Azores. These 'commerce raiders' built in Liverpool did serious damage to Northern trade during the War. The ships were usually sold to the Confederacy through intermediaries. A sham sale to China in April 1863 drew from *Harper's Weekly* an outburst headed 'British Pirates': 'Two so-called Chinese frigates have been launched in Liverpool by Mr. Laird, builder of the *Alabama*. All the indications point to a general conspiracy in England against the United States merchant navy. Every British Official from Earl Russell downwards is possessed with the idea that now or never is the time to drive all American ships from the face of the ocean.'

[9]

It is not surprising that tempers rose; but thanks to the patience and skill of two excellent diplomats, Mr. Adams in London and Lord Lyons in Washington, they were kept below boiling point and the matter of the Liverpool-built privateers, although a continuing irritant, was never allowed seriously to threaten war between the two countries.

The *Alabama* should never have been released to the Confederacy. This was a mistake made by officials and not a deliberate act of hostility by the British Government. After the War England made amends to the tune of £3,100,000 which was paid to the United States in compensation for damage done by the *Alabama* and her sister raiders.

The dangerous situation that arose in 1863 was due to the fact that Mr. Laird had now embarked upon a much more serious project — namely, the construction of two armoured ships of war for the Confederacy. Officially they were being built for a French purchaser acting for the Turkish Viceroy of Egypt; but it was 'an open secret' that they were destined for the Confederacy and Mr. Adams went to great pains to prove his case. As the ships neared completion, tension increased. Mr. Seward sent repeated warnings to Lord Russell. Finally, 'under plain threat of war', Russell, on holiday in Scotland, wrote to Palmerston advising him to stop the 'rams'. The Government then intervened and Mr. Laird was ordered to sell the two ships to the British Navy. The ships which gave

FOREIGN NEWS.

ENGLAND.

THE REBEL RAMS TO BE DETAINED.

WE have the very important information that the British Government has decided to detain Laird's rebel iron rams. This fact has thrown a decided gloom over the rebels and their sympathizers in England.

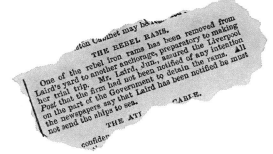

Cuttings from *Harper's Weekly*, issues October 3, October 10, and November 3, 1863 and opposite are drawings of the rebel rams.

THE REISSUE OF

HARPER'S WEEKLY.

A JOURNAL OF CIVILIZATION.

VOL. VII.—No. 364.]   NEW YORK, SATURDAY, DECEMBER 19, 1863.   [SINGLE COPIES SIX CENTS.
[$3.00 PER YEAR IN ADVANCE.

Entered according to Act of Congress, in the Year 1863, by Harper & Brothers, in the Clerk's Office of the District Court for the Southern District of New York.

THE LAIRD RAM "EL MONASSIR," SEIZED BY THE BRITISH GOVERNMENT.—[SEE NEXT PAGE.]

THE LAIRD RAM "EL TOUSSON," SEIZED BY THE BRITISH GOVERNMENT.—[SEE NEXT PAGE.]

all this trouble started their lives with the Turkish names, *El Tousson* and *El Monassir*, and finished as H.M.S. *Scorpion* and H.M.S. *Wivern*.

It must be said that, in spite of a strident press and a public opinion hostile to the North, the Liberal Government of Palmerston acted on the whole with correct neutrality towards the Union. In this it was supported by Disraeli and other leading Conservatives in the Opposition. In Northern eyes, however, neutrality was not enough. In Boston and New England the men whom Yates Thompson met in 1863 were deeply troubled about England's attitude. *The Times* newspaper was particularly hostile to the Union. 'There has been no more constant, false, venomous and unscrupulous enemy of this country than the London *Times*', commented *Harper's Weekly* in February 1863 and this was no overstatement.5 It is painful today to read about the attitudes and assertions of many leading Englishmen at that time. Lord Robert Cecil (later the great Lord Salisbury) publicly expressed his friendship for the South as a good trading partner and his antagonism to the North as a business rival.

There were some important exceptions. One of the few eminent Englishmen moved to sympathy with the North was the poet, Tennyson; and the North

5. Charles Francis Adams, American Minister in London, writing in January 1862 to his brother-in-law Edward Everett, declared that 'it is impossible to hope for any fair dealing [from *The Times*]. Its policy is to secure the division of the Union as an essential security to the peace of Europe and the preponderance of Great Britain.'

W. H. Russell, *The Times* war correspondent of Crimean fame, had been assigned to Washington. In August 1861 he watched the Battle of Bull Run through opera glasses from a point of vantage with a party of ladies and members of Congress. His dispatches occupied seven columns in *The Times* of August 9, 1861, and were accompanied by a most scathing leading article. Russell's detailed account of the rout of United Federal troops, and their panic flight back to Washington, dwelt upon some of the shocking episodes that he had witnessed and these passages were copiously quoted in American newspapers. Russell was denounced as an enemy of the Union and a memorial was presented to Seward calling for his expulsion.

On December 5 of the same year when war between England and America seemed near as a result of the *Trent* affair, the manager of *The Times* wrote to Russell: 'If there is war the scene of your operations will be Canada. Your first step will be to place yourself in safety on board a British ship and I take it for granted that Lord Lyons will allow you to attach yourself *pro tem* to his embassy. He, I should think, will go to Halifax unless his orders are to come home at once; and I know of no better place than Halifax for you in the first instance.'

In July 1862 the *Spectator* observed that '*The Times* which is aware that its articles weigh heavily in America, writes every now and then as if it wanted war'. In 1862 when Lee was gaining victories over the Army of the Potomac *The Times* declared: 'Should it appear that the army of McClellan has been so totally defeated as to be incapable of resuming offensive operations, then the propriety of treating the Confederate as an independent people may be justly discussed by the British Cabinet.' (From *The History of the Times 1841–1884*, Volume II, published in 1939.)

had two steadfast supporters in those famous agitators, Richard Cobden* and John Bright. Inside and outside Parliament they championed the Northern cause.

In his biography of John Bright, Professor G. M. Trevelyan* describes how, when the press and the leaders of 'oligarchic England' supported the Confederacy, 'Bright and his friends roused the unenfranchised masses to proclaim their sympathy with freedom across the Atlantic'.

The cotton workers of Lancashire, unemployed and nearly starving because the Northern blockade of Southern ports prevented cotton from reaching the Lancashire mills, made public demonstrations in support of the North.

Before the Civil War, Bright had met Senator Charles Sumner and during the War he kept him informed about the movement of English opinion through letters written also for the eye of President Lincoln. Bright's letter to Sumner urging moderation at the climax of the *Trent* affair was read aloud at the meeting of Lincoln's Cabinet in December 1861 when the fateful decision was made to allow Mason and Slidell to continue their journey to Europe.

It is easy to imagine the atmosphere in Boston when Yates Thompson arrived there in July 1863. Trollope was in Boston the year before and this is how he describes it:

'The bitterness towards England amounts almost to a passion. The name of an Englishman has been made a byword of reproach. I must confess that I have not been so proud of the tone of all our people at home. Some of us never tire of abusing the Americans, and calling them names, for having allowed themselves to be driven into this Civil War; but I do not remember to have seen any statement as to what the Northern states should have done. For their part, they cannot understand that we should not wish them to be successful in putting down a rebellion. I left Boston with a sad feeling in my heart that a quarrel was imminent between England and the United States.'[6]

Boston had many English associations, and Bostonians were particularly sensitive to English opinion. Reports from friends in England brought nothing but evidence of dislike and criticism. Edward Everett himself, Yates Thompson's Boston host, said some very harsh things about England in the lecture that Trollope heard him deliver in 1862. Resentments against England burnt deep and lasted for a long time after the War was over. Nevertheless, Yates Thompson encountered nothing but kindness and friendship in the America of 1863, not only in Boston, but everywhere his travels took him. He was certainly a keen partisan of the North when he arrived in America and there was

6. From *North America* by Anthony Trollope, 1862.

no mistaking where his sympathies lay. He was a friendly and a shrewd young man, but he was deeply touched by the warmth of his welcome in America at that difficult time.

He transcribed into his Diary copies of letters that he sent to the *Daily News* in London as he went along. They were well published, and they show their writer as an active unofficial propagandist for the Union. It is not to be wondered at that when he returned home he was determined to do what he could to dispel the dangerous ignorance of his own countrymen in all matters relating to America. In 1864 he went about England lecturing on the Civil War, an impassioned spokesman for the North and a hater of slavery. But in an imaginative attempt to do something positive to improve Anglo-American understanding he met with a rebuff from Cambridge, his beloved University.

The American Historical Review of April 1918 tells this story under the title 'The Thompson Readership, a forgotten episode of Academic History'.

'A comparatively unknown and youthful graduate of Cambridge University, Henry Yates Thompson (B.A. Trinity 1862), son of a wealthy Liverpool banker, came to the United States in 1863. Introduced to Edward Everett of Boston, and through him to other Americans, young Thompson obtained glimpses of Boston and Cambridge society, and was enabled to travel under peculiarly favourable auspices all over the country. In politics, already an advanced Liberal, and advocate of the extension of the franchise in England, an admirer of Cobden and Bright, open minded, impressionable, and deeply interested in the success of the Union cause here, he became convinced through his visit of the widespread and deplorable ignorance of the United States which characterised especially the upper classes of his countrymen. On December 24, 1864, Mr. Thompson addressed a letter to Edward Everett in which he propounded a cherished plan. "My wish", he wrote, "is to endow a Lectureship, or as we call it at Lincoln's Inn a Readership, at Harvard University, its object being the delivery of a biennial course of twelve lectures during a residence of one term at Cambridge in England on the 'History and Political Institutions of the United States of America', such reader to be appointed biennially by the President and Fellows of Harvard University (subject to the veto in each case of the Vice-Chancellor of Cambridge), and his sole qualifications to be American citizenship and the opinion of his appointers that he is a fit person to deliver such a course."'

Unfortunately for 'young Thompson' his project proved to be long ahead of its time. A bitter controversy was ignited at Cambridge University. It dragged on through the whole of 1865 and makes strange reading today. It was not until February 1866 that the proposal was publicly discussed in the Senate of the University. *The Times* commented: 'a great many flysheets on the subject have been circulated: a great many non-residents came up to vote: the strength of the opposition was mainly due to a fear lest the lectures should be a means of diffusing Unitarian opinions'. It was further suggested that the Harvard lecturer if appointed would introduce notions of 'republicanism' or even of 'democracy'. On February 22, 1866, the Yates Thompson lectureship was voted out in the Senate by 107 votes against 81 to the mortification of its sponsor and the embarrassment of Harvard. Leslie Stephen*, the father of Virginia Woolf, then a Cambridge don and in due time an eminent philosopher and man of letters, visited Harvard in July 1863 at the same time as Yates Thompson. He too espoused the cause of the North and condemned slavery. He supported the Cambridge lectureship proposal, but to no avail; the day after the vote (February 23, 1866) he wrote to his Harvard friend, James Russell Lowell*, who at a later date became American Minister in London:

The voting body — our Senate — consists of everyone who has taken the degree of M.A. . . . Directly I went into the Senate House yesterday I saw at a glance that we were done for. The district round Cambridge is generously supplied with parsons who can be brought up when the Church is in danger. Beings whom I recognized at once by their rustic appearance, ancient and shiny silk gowns, elaborate white ties and shabby hats instead of college caps, were swarming all around me. When once the Church is having its foundations sapped, and that by an American democrat, it would be easier to argue with a herd of swine than British parsons.

Lowell replied: 'I doubt if the Lectureship could have done much good. England CAN'T like America; and I doubt if I could were I an Englishman.'

In my great uncle's papers I found a letter written in July 1865 by the Rev. W. O. White, a Unitarian minister, who was his kindly host at Keene, New Hampshire, in 1863. 'Perhaps,' he said, 'had your proposition been made some six years before the Civil War, it might have been kindlier met in England. But, had you been old enough to make it then, you would not have thought America half so well worth being informed about, as she had not then tested so unmistakably the framework of her government or the spirit of her people.'

It was not until 1922 that the first Chair of American History was established at an English University, this time at Oxford instead of Cambridge. The first lecture was delivered by Professor S. E. Morison of Harvard. After describing the failure of the proposed Yates Thompson Readership he said:

'What other result could have been expected? The Church and the governing classes then had their backs to the wall facing the onward march of manhood suffrage. The mere existence of the American Republic, of democracy victorious and triumphant, was bad enough. But to have this thing taught and propagated at Cambridge by a nominee of that Cardinal's College of Unitarianism, the President and Fellows of Harvard, was too much.'

I discovered in my great-uncle's papers that there had been an attempt by Cambridge in 1907 to persuade him to revive his offer. He wrote to the Vice-Chancellor of Cambridge University from Portman Square on May 16, 1907:

Referring to your letter of March last in which you asked me whether I was inclined to renew the offer which I made 42 years ago to endow an American lectureship at Cambridge, and to our subsequent conversation on the subject, I have now to say that, on reflection, I have come to the conclusion that the offer could not be advantageously renewed in the form in which I made it in 1865, for the following reasons:

(1) It was ill received by our Masters of Arts at that time and the well meant intervention of Harvard University was rather bluntly refused. This would make it a little difficult to ask the assistance of Harvard in the nomination of lecturers now.

(2) At that time there was a crying need for better information in England about American institutions. The Civil War was only just ended and ignorance of America had all but involved our government in that war on the side of the South which would have been such a great calamity. No such special need exists now.

(3) Lectureships have multiplied in Cambridge and it is, as I am informed, sometimes difficult for an outside lecturer to secure an audience in sufficient numbers. It would be sad to bring over a lecturer from America and then to have no good audience for his course of lectures.

These reasons make me adverse to any renewal of the offer of 1865. There is besides the idea expressed in the French lines:

> *'et souvenez vous bien*
> *Qu'un diner rechauffé ne valait jamais rien.'*

His discovery of America in 1863 was one of the major events in my great-uncle's life. It remained fresh in his memory right to the end of it, and he used to describe the Battle of Chattanooga to me as if it had happened the week before.

The Diary gives a good impression of the enormous scale of the War, and the immense size of the country. There had been nothing on quite such a scale before. When Grant took the field as General-in-Chief in 1864 the total strength of the armies of the Union, spread over a vast area, was of the order of 900,000 men. It is probable that during the period of the War about half a million Americans on each side were killed or died from wounds or disease in the military service or were taken prisoner. From first to last some 3,000,000 Americans saw military service. Until the 1914–18 War this was probably the most bloody struggle humanity had ever known.

Highgate Literary & Scientific Institution.

Jan. 3rd,
CHRISTMAS ENTERTAINMENT,
COMIC SCENES AND COMIC SONGS,
By MR. EDWARD DALE.
LATE OF THE ROYAL COLOSSEUM, LONDON.
To commence at 7 o'clock.   Tickets—Members, and Children under 12 years of age, 6d ;
Visitors' Tickets, 1s. each.

SPRING COURSE OF LECTURES, 1865.

ON TUESDAY EVENINGS, AT EIGHT O'CLOCK.

Jan. 31st,
THE BATTLE OF CHATTANOOGA,
By H. Y. THOMPSON, ESQ.—(an Eye-witness.)

Feb. 14th,
A NEW MAP OF ASIA,
By LORD WILLIAM HAY, B.C.S.

Feb. 28th,
TWO HOURS WITH THE HUMOURISTS,
WITH ILLUSTRATIONS FROM MANY AUTHORS.
BY J. H. SIDDONS, Esq.

March 14th,
A MUSICAL ENTERTAINMENT, ENTITLED
A SHAKESPERIAN RAMBLE,
By MR. HARE, (assisted by several Talented Artistes).

March 22nd,
THE ANNUAL MEETING,
To receive the Annual Report, Elect Officers, &c.   To this meeting Strangers are not admitted.

March 28th,
THE POETRY OF LIFE,
By W. J. R. COTTON, Esq.

April 25th,
ON SLATE : ITS SOURCES AND USES,
By F. E. BODKIN, Esq.

MEMBERS are entitled to a Free Admission—transferable by WRITTEN ORDER—and ASSOCIATES
to Personal Admission to the Lectures.
Tickets for Non-Subscribers can be obtained at the Institution.
W. P. BODKIN, Hon. Sec.

Henry Yates Thompson gave lectures in 1864 and 1865 on his American experiences.

Yates Thompson's experience on the battlefield of Chattanooga gave him a distaste for war that never left him. Many years later he was a strong opponent of the South African War, and he told me that a number of London drawing rooms were closed to him in consequence. He gave a lecture to the boys of Harrow, his old school, on the Battle of Chattanooga on March 7, 1865, before his friend, the headmaster, Dr. Butler. After a lively account of the battle he said:

'I set out to describe a battle; but the battle is not yet over when the victory is won. True the victory was very complete. General Bragg* and his army were gone in sudden flight from their strong positions. The siege of Chattanooga was raised. The victors captured six or seven thousand prisoners and many batteries of guns.

'We have seen something of the pomp of war. Now look at the reverse of the medal – seven or eight thousand killed or wounded men lying out in those late November woods, a protest of suffering humanity against the prodigious wickedness of war. The impression left on me by my walks the next day through those blood-stained woods (and if ever there was, as Dante has it, a *selva selvaggia ed aspra e forte che nel pensier rinova la paura*, it was there in my lonely walks over the battlefield) fixed a conviction in my mind, a conviction of the absolute and essential wickedness of those who talk lightly of war and still more of those who lightly begin a war. Surely, if those reckless men, who fired in 1861 the first gun on Fort Sumter which began the awful tragedy, had dreamed of one half of the woes in which they would involve their fellow countrymen, they would rather have cut off their right hands than have raised them in that outrageous act.'

Mr. Bruce Catton refers to the dreadful effect of the new weapons coming into use in the Civil War. 'The rifled musket', he writes, 'not only had a greater range and accuracy than anything soldiers had ever used before; it made an uncommonly nasty wound – a good deal worse in most cases than one inflicted by today's rifle and infinitely worse than that of the round ball fired by the old smoothbore. The ghastly number of amputations performed at all field hospitals (the hideous number of severed arms and legs lying by the hospital tents) took place because when one of those soft lead bullets hit a bone it usually splintered so horribly that no medical magic could save the limb.[7] My great-uncle never forgot the screams of the wounded on the battlefield at Chattanooga.

After his death in 1928 Yates Thompson's papers lay in a cupboard for many years unread. At last I have found time to read his American diaries of 1863 and the letters kept with them. This has encouraged me to improve my own inadequate knowledge of this heroic period of American history. Many millions of words have been written about the Civil War and there can be little new to

7. From *Mr. Lincoln's Army* by Bruce Catton, 1951.

discover. But the freshness and unaffectedness of my great-uncle's Diary may appeal to Americans however familiar they are with their own history. The English are still shamefully ignorant of American history and it is for their benefit that I have tried to provide some background setting for the diaries. With this purpose I have written an introduction to each of the three notebooks of the diaries and I have provided some footnotes. I hope American readers will not find this unduly wearisome.

The diaries cover six months – from July 10 to December 13, 1863. Their climax is the spectacular and decisive Battle of Chattanooga which was fought on November 23, 24, and 25. They are written in ink in three notebooks: there is also a small pocket book entered in pencil during the Battle of Chattanooga which I have interposed into the third notebook. There are a number of rough pencil sketches in the notebooks a few of which have been reproduced. In addition to Yates Thompson's letters to the *Daily News* of London which are part of the diaries, I have inserted at the appropriate dates some of his letters to members of the Thompson family in Liverpool, his father and mother, his two aunts, his sister Meggie, later married to the Dean of Lichfield, and his two younger brothers, Sam and Rodie, the latter being my grandfather.

Book I starts in Boston and ends in New Haven, Connecticut.

Book II starts in New York; it includes a visit to slave plantations in eastern Maryland and to wartime Washington; then a journey from Washington by rail to Chicago and further west, down the Mississippi by river steamer to St. Louis, Missouri, and on by rail to Louisville, Kentucky.

Book III starts in Nashville, capital of Tennessee, and covers the Battle of Chattanooga and the journey back to New York.

At the beginning of this Foreword I quoted a letter to William Everett written in Turin in June 1863 before the American journey. Here is another, written in New York in December when the journey was over.

December 10, 1863
Brevoort House,
New York

Having traversed this country from Pilot Knob to the Isle of Shoals, from the slave farms of eastern Maryland to the Federal camps in Northern Georgia, from the prairies of Minnesota to where Vallandigham* mingles his tears with the icy waters of the Detroit river, I am coming to Boston some day next week and staying there till the departure of the Canada *on the 23rd inst.*

I cannot tell you how much I have been entertained by every part of my journey.

[19]

All that I have time to tell you now is that by a great piece of good luck I got to Chatta-nooga the day before Grant began to move his army on November 23, and witnessed from Fort Wood the three days' fighting which ended in Bragg's retreat from Missionary Ridge and Lookout Mountain. The newspaper correspondents cannot exaggerate the splendour of the whole affair as a military pageant. It was warfare in its most attractive form of hard and successful fighting under an Italian sky in a most picturesque part of the country.

I hope your father was none the worse for his great speech at Gettysburg. Please give my best regards to him and also to Mrs. Wise[8] if she is still at home.

In February 1864 Yates Thompson wrote to William Everett from Liverpool about his lecture tour in England:

... each time after I had praised up your side well, the chief inhabitant of the place present got up and presented the Southern case, which gave some zest to the per-formance. But people here are being a good deal converted on the subject of North and South. Certain truths are beginning faintly to dawn on peoples' minds. Liverpool, however, is still a good deal the other way. Next month there is to be a grand Southern bazaar here, which will no doubt be a success as there are some very energetic Southern ladies here and some beautiful young Creole ladies are coming from Paris to sell at the stalls.

In September 1865 he wrote about his troubles over the Cambridge Readership:

I am going for a few days to Cambridge about my Lectureship scheme. I was delighted by the letter from Dr. Hill* to Cookson (Vice-Chancellor of Cambridge), but do not feel at all confident of the thing being accepted. They talk of its being a 'democratic propaganda', etc. — as if the Harvard dons were red republicans! I can imagine no more delightful thing than having a live Yankee lecturing those musty dons at Cam-bridge.

Twenty years later we find Yates Thompson inviting William Everett to contribute articles to the *Pall Mall Gazette* on the American political scene: 'I write at once because you may have more leisure for this kind of thing before term commences at Harvard. Such an article should contain 1,500 to 2,000 words which keeps it under two columns.'

My great-uncle always remembered the kindness of the Americans he met in 1863. One of his last letters to William Everett is dated March 7, 1908:

8. Edward Everett's daughter.

On board R.M.S. Baltic *: to America again. My two original first hosts in America — you and the Rev. Mr. White, then of Keene, New Hampshire, are both still flourishing after forty years, which is very creditable to all three of us. How I wish we could be paying a visit to your father in Summer Street, Boston, as in 1863. How astonished he would be at the changes.*

We have just made the Nantucket Light. *So I am feeling quite at home!*

BOOK I

JULY 10 – SEPTEMBER 14

Editor's Introduction

THE FIRST BOOK of the diaries opens on July 10, 1863, at the house of Edward Everett in Summer Street, Boston, and it gives a picture of New England in the middle year of the Civil War. It closes with an entry on September 14 at New Haven, Connecticut.

The New England renaissance was at high noon in 1863. The dogmas of Calvinistic Puritanism had given ground before freer systems of thought and expression. The Unitarian movement had loosened the old disciplines and a new type of theology was preached from the pulpits of Boston. Ralph Waldo Emerson had resigned his ministry in 1832 because he no longer felt inclined to administer the sacrament. This is sometimes taken as about the date when free religious debate and argument became accepted in New England. In a whole number of directions there was a quickening of activity; and Boston was established as the intellectual centre of America.

At Cambridge on the edge of Boston, Harvard College, America's oldest university, with a good classical tradition, developed important schools of history and literature. Prescott and Motley were historians of the first rank. Ticknor, Longfellow, and Lowell became in turn professors of literature. Enthusiasts of new philosophies called themselves Transcendentalists, each seeking his own individual approach to truth.

In the more traditional New England spirit a great reforming movement grew up in the 1830s seeking the abolition of slavery. This movement reached its greatest intensity in the 1850s and became one of the more important factors leading up to the Civil War.

Boston also became the headquarters of the school of American classical oratory of which Edward Everett was the acknowledged leader. Under the sponsorship of Edward Everett, a former President of Harvard, my great-uncle

[25]

met leading members of 'the Brahmin caste of New England', so named by Oliver Wendell Holmes*, who was one of them. Being a fine classical scholar, he was not entirely out of place in such company. But they were a formidable, if rather self-conscious, group of intellectuals; and he admits in his diaries to having been 'frightened' when called upon to speak in front of them at a gathering of the Harvard alumni.

In 1863 Edward Everett was seventy years old and he was nearing the end of his career. He had filled many important positions and during his short period as Secretary of State he had proved himself a competent administrator. He was still a national figure in 1863, but he was no longer taken seriously as a politician. His political judgement faltered when he ran in the 1860 election as vice-presidential candidate for the Third Party, the party of compromise. Lincoln carried the Republicans to victory and the party of compromise came a poor third in the electoral vote.

There was something lacking in Edward Everett, due, it has been said, to a strain of timidity in his character. Today he would be called an appeaser. In his anxiety to prevent the conflict between North and South he was prepared to come to terms with slavery. His distinguished brother-in-law, Charles Francis Adams, United States Minister in London, said of him: 'He was stuff not good enough to wear in rainy weather, though bright enough in sunshine.' But when Secession finally became a reality he cast away all his hesitations and doubts and became a tireless advocate for the War. He wore himself out in aid of the national call to arms to save the Union.

Edward Everett at the time of Yates Thompson's Boston visit was still greatly in demand as an orator. In this skill he was a professional. After his death, at the instance of his son William, four large volumes were published containing his speeches and lectures delivered on a great variety of themes and occasions. Anthony Trollope heard him in Boston in 1862 and wrote in his *North America*:

'The whole thing is done in a grand style. Music is introduced. The lecturer stands on a large raised platform. Mr. Everett lectures without any book or paper before him and continues from first to last as if the words come to him on the spur of the moment. It is known, however, that it is his practice to prepare his orations with great care and commit them entirely to memory, as does an actor. Indeed he repeats the same lecture again and again, I am told, without the change of a word or of an action. Some among his countrymen have said that there is an affectation in the motion of his hands, and that the intended pathos of his voice sometimes approaches too near the precipice, over which the fall is so deep and rapid,

Edward Everett, November 1863 (from *Edward Everett at Gettysburg*, Massachusetts Historical Society).

and at the bottom of which lies absolute ridicule. Judging for myself, I did not find it so. His power of oratory is very wonderful, his power of delivery very marvellous.'

It was a great occasion for Edward Everett when, on November 19, 1863, he made the official speech dedicating part of the battlefield of Gettysburg as a national cemetery. He was seventy; and he spoke faultlessly from memory for two hours on a windy November day before an audience of 12,000 people. His speech had taken weeks to prepare and it began thus:

'Standing beneath this serene sky, overlooking the broad fields now reposing from the labour of the waning year, the mighty Alleghanies dimly towering above us, the graves of our brethren beneath our feet, it is with hesitation that I raise my poor voice to break the eloquent silence of God and nature.'

Then, with dramatic intonation and gesture, he recorded the customs of ancient Athens, the history of European civilization, the military campaigns leading to Gettysburg and, in profuse and accurate detail, the part played by each unit of the Union army on the battlefield – with this concluding sentence:

'Wheresoever throughout the civilized world the accounts of this great warfare are read, and down to the latest period of recorded time, in the glorious annals of our common country there will be no brighter page than that which relates to the Battle of Gettysburg.'

Then Lincoln spoke for two minutes and delivered what is now known as 'the Gettysburg speech'.

'No one now ever reads the words of the polished orator'; but Lincoln's 'words, cut in marble in our noblest tomb, may yet outlive the stone on which they are inscribed.'[1] Yet Edward Everett, as an observer on the platform said, 'spoke perfectly'. He had done exactly what was expected of him. At the time Lincoln's speech was little noticed;[2] and it was only at a later date that the power

1. From *The Epic of America* by James Truslaw Adams, 1932.
2. On November 20, 1863, Edward Everett wrote to Lincoln: 'Permit me', he said, 'to express my great admiration of the thoughts expressed by you, with such eloquent simplicity and appropriateness, at the consecration of the Cemetery. I should be glad if I could flatter myself that I came to the central idea of the occasion in two hours as you did in two minutes.' Lincoln replied on the same day: 'In our respective parts yesterday, you could not have been excused to make a short address, nor I a long one. I am pleased to know that, in your judgement, the little I did say was not entirely a failure. Of course I knew Mr. Everett would not fail, and yet, while the whole discourse was eminently satisfactory, and will be of great value, there were passages in it which transcended my expectations.' ('Edward Everett at Gettysburg', published by The Massachusetts Historical Society, Boston, 1963.)

and beauty of his words came to be recognized. Compared with the elaborate oratory so popular in his day Lincoln's simpler style was strikingly original.

Edward Everett died in January 1865 and at the invitation of the City of Boston Richard Henry Dana*, who as an abolitionist had opposed him, delivered the funeral oration – at immense length and in a style that would have gladdened the old orator's heart.

'When Mr. Seward, at the seat of Government, by order of the President announced to the whole country the death of Edward Everett, and requested that all honour should be paid to his memory, at home or abroad wherever the national authority was recognized, all the people said Amen! For fifty years, year by year, Mr. Everett has submitted orations, speeches, diplomatic letters, essays and lectures to the judgement of his age.

I cannot close a notice of his public life without alluding to that test by which posterity will judge American statesmen of the last twenty years – the question, with what wisdom and courage have they met the subject of slavery? Being of the number of those who disapprove, nay, who condemn, the course of concession and compromise to which Mr. Everett inclined, I feel the more bound to render him, on this point, the justice that I think his due. It was always his belief that if secession were attempted the American people would have before them but this alternative – disintegration or Civil War. I think Mr. Everett knew the nature of slavery, that he felt its injustice. He is fairly entitled to be judged as a peace man. But when at length the blow was struck he threw the whole weight of his character, influence and powers into the scale for the national life.'

So ended the career of my great-uncle's kindly host in Boston.

What happened to his son, William Everett, who was directly responsible for the Boston visit? He tried hard to follow in his father's footsteps – joined the Unitarian ministry, studied the law, practised oratory and essayed politics. But it all came to nothing; and, after a period as assistant professor in Latin at Harvard, he became headmaster of the Adams Academy at Quincy, an institution which saw its end during his administration. He became increasingly eccentric as he got older. But my great-uncle, a loyal friend, maintained a regular correspondence with him for more than forty-five years. He died in 1910.

Yates Thompson was privileged to start his American travels under the hospitable roof of the Everett family. Here he heard the abolitionists mentioned with disfavour. There were divisions still in Boston. But, as the War progressed and as Lincoln moved towards emancipation, abolition became more popular. In the early days there had been recurrent crises and strife. Extreme abolitionists

[28]

went in danger of their lives in Boston and in 1835 William Lloyd Garrison* was very nearly lynched.

Yates Thompson came to America already a hater of slavery and he sought out the abolitionists. He did not see William Lloyd Garrison; and when he

An advertisement for *Uncle Tom's Cabin* by Harriet Beecher Stowe.

called on Harriet Beecher Stowe at Andover he found that only her husband was at home. But he was luckier when he paid a visit to Wendell Phillips*, the most distinguished and eloquent of the spokesmen for abolition.

Garrison had founded the New England Anti-Slavery Society in 1831. In his paper *The Liberator* he never ceased to thunder against the evils of slavery in

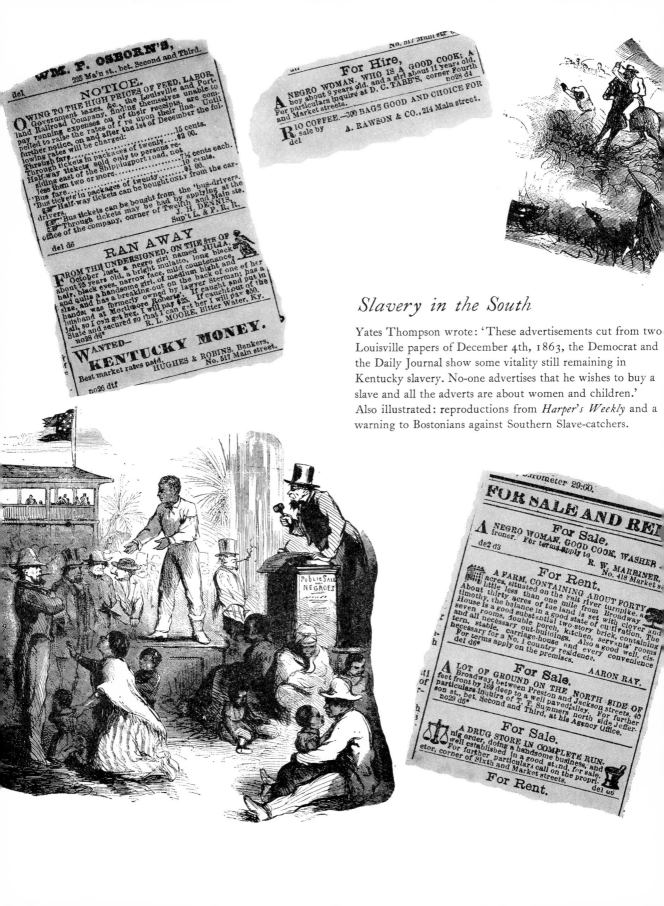

Slavery in the South

Yates Thompson wrote: 'These advertisements cut from two Louisville papers of December 4th, 1863, the Democrat and the Daily Journal show some vitality still remaining in Kentucky slavery. No-one advertises that he wishes to buy a slave and all the adverts are about women and children.'
Also illustrated: reproductions from *Harper's Weekly* and a warning to Bostonians against Southern Slave-catchers.

CAUTION!!

COLORED PEOPLE

OF BOSTON, ONE & ALL,

You are hereby respectfully CAUTIONED and advised, to avoid conversing with the

Watchmen and Police Officers of Boston,

For since the recent ORDER OF THE MAYOR & ALDERMEN, they are empowered to act as

KIDNAPPERS

AND

Slave Catchers,

And they have already been actually employed in KIDNAPPING, CATCHING, AND KEEPING SLAVES. Therefore, if you value your LIBERTY, and the *Welfare of the Fugitives* among you, *Shun* them in every possible manner, as so many *HOUNDS* on the track of the most unfortunate of your race.

Keep a Sharp Look Out for KIDNAPPERS, and have TOP EYE open.

the South, until at last in 1865 he was able to lock up his presses in the knowledge that his work was done. Harriet Beecher Stowe had been urged to write something 'which would make the whole nation feel what an accursed thing slavery is'. This she did in 1852 in the form of a novel, *Uncle Tom's Cabin*, which is believed to have had a greater impact upon opinion than any other novel ever written.

Wendell Phillips was a brilliant agitator and a passionate speaker. He was dedicated to abolition and laboured continuously and fearlessly on its behalf despite bitter and sometimes violent opposition. But he was himself a violent man. Trollope heard him speak at Boston and wrote:

'The doctrine he preached was one of rapine, bloodshed and social destruction. There is no being so venomous, so bloodthirsty, as a professed philanthropist; and when the philanthropist's ardour lies negro-wards it then assumes the deepest die of venom and bloodthirstyness. There are four millions of slaves in the Southern states – and Mr. Phillips would emancipate these at a blow and set them loose upon the soil to tear their masters and destroy each other.'3

The abolitionists stirred the country, both North and South. They aroused the conscience of the North and goaded the South to the most bitter resentment. They hardened the division between North and South and kept slavery in the forefront of public debate. The factors leading to the War were deeprooted and complex. But slavery was a fundamental issue. Lincoln saw this clearly enough and he said so in unforgettable words: 'A house divided against itself cannot stand. I believe this Government cannot endure permanently half slave half free.'4

It will be noted in the diaries that Yates Thompson during his travels in New England was assiduously reading Olmsted's *Cotton Kingdom*. This is an important book and Frederick Law Olmsted was an interesting man. He was born in Hartford, Connecticut, in 1822 and died in 1903. He was commissioned in the 1850s by the *New York Daily Times* to travel over the Southern States and write articles describing 'the peculiar institution' of African slavery in practice. He wrote three travel books based upon these articles and in 1861 an English publisher (Sampson Low Son & Co.) condensed the three books into a single book of two volumes entitled *The Cotton Kingdom, a traveller's observations on cotton and slavery in the American Slave States*.5 It became a classic of the same

3. From *North America* by Anthony Trollope, 1862.
4. From a speech by Lincoln in the 1858 public debate with Stephen A. Douglas in the Illinois election for the Senate.
5. Republished in 1969 by the Modern Library, New York.

sort as Arthur Young's *Travels in France*,[6] compiled on the eve of the French Revolution. Both books show the same keenness of observation and the same gift for accurate, yet vivid, reporting.

Olmsted in his investigations describes with detached impartiality exactly what he saw in the slave States. Abolitionists criticized him for dwelling, in their view, excessively on the economic aspects of slavery without condemning its moral aspect. But he had set out in his travels determined to be fair to the slave-owners. In his own words he did what he could 'to prevent the pot boiling over'. The painstaking impartiality of his writing makes all the more effective what is, in fact if not in intention, a devastating condemnation of 'chattel slavery', a system that the Southern States were fighting to preserve and, if possible, to extend.

It is difficult to assess the influence of Olmsted's writing in England. *The Cotton Kingdom* was published there after the War had started and pro-South sentiment was strong. But in America his books had a great impact. Lowell wrote to Olmsted saying: 'I have learned more about the South from your books than from all others put together, and I valued them the more as an American who can be patient and accurate is so rare a phenomenon!' It is hard to give an impression of this book without quoting from it. I give a single, but telling, sample:

'The cash value of a slave for sale is considered among the surest elements of estimating a planter's worth. A slave woman is commonly esteemed most for the qualities which give value to a brood-mare. This is made constantly apparent to me. A slave-owner told me that in the states of Maryland, Virginia, Kentucky and Missouri, as much attention is given to the breeding and growth of negroes as to that of horses and mules. Planters command their girls and women (married or unmarried) to have children; and a great many negro girls are sold off because they do not have children. A breeding woman is worth one-fourth more than one that does not breed.'

Olmsted was a remarkable man in a number of ways. His profession was that of landscape architect and in 1857 he was made Superintendent of New York's new Central Park. He designed the grounds of the Capitol in Washington and, with his Boston friend Charles Eliot Norton*, whom we meet in Yates Thompson's Diary, he ran a successful campaign to prevent the extinction of the Niagara Falls. At the beginning of the Civil War he was appointed General Secretary of the Sanitary Commission, precursor of the American Red Cross, which grew into a huge organization for succouring the wounded on the battlefields. It was through the Sanitary Commission that Yates Thompson was enabled to reach the battlefield of Chattanooga.

6. Written by Arthur Young after a tour of France on horseback, May to November 1887.

The Diary

JULY 10 – SEPTEMBER 14

Friday July 10 1863 Summer Street Boston

I hereby institute my American diary, which I declar[e]
strictly private, only not under lock & key because [the]
key of my locked book is left at home.

I have just visited with W. Everett ye State House [of]
where ye Adjutant General Mr. Schouler whom W. E[verett]
as "General" shewed me a Springfield rifle, upon[?]
because the parts of one & any of them coincid[e]
part of another — 11 lbs weight — 2 inches longer the[?]
with a wad place in ye stock & low sights. Th[e]
goodnatured & grizzly. Went into ye Senate
I have today seen 2 statues of General [Washington]
two autograph letters of his. Chantrey's
classicalism. The other in ye Athen[aeum]
G. Washin. & was writing sweetly to Mr[s]
[after]wards married. He is very fide[?]
(somewhat elephantine.
[to?] a Mrs. Stockton
[?] federal in

FRIDAY, JULY 10, 1863

Boston, Massachusetts

I hereby institute my American diary, which I declare strictly private, and only not under lock and key because the key of my locked book is left at home.

I have just visited with Mr. Everett the State House of Boston where the Adjutant-General Mr. Schouler* whom Mr. Everett addressed as 'General,' showed me a Springfield rifle superior to the Enfield[1] because the parts of one and any of them coincide with a part of another—11 lbs weight—2 inches longer than the Enfield, with a wad plate in the stock and low sights. The Adjutant-General was big, good-natured, and grizzly. Went into the Senate House : forty Senators present.

I have today seen 2 statues of General Washington and read two autograph letters of his. Chauntrey's statue a good example of classicalism. The other in the Atheneum. In 1756 G. Washington was writing sweetly to Mrs. Martha Custis whom he afterwards married. He is very polite, but his jokes, as Mr. Everett observed, somewhat elephantine.

1. The Enfield rifle was made in England: the South purchased 200,000 rifles from Europe during the Civil War, mostly Enfields from England.

From Edward Everett's diary: July 10

Mr. Stephen of Trinity Hall Cam. & Dr. O. W. Holmes dine with us to meet our young friend Thompson.— Judge Warren called in the Evening.

Mr. Thompson a fellow-student of Willy arrived in the Steamer this morning, & came to stay with us for a few days.

SATURDAY, JULY 11

Boston

9.30 a.m. Have just come upstairs from a conversation with Mr. Edward Everett. He wrote to Mr. Seward after Fort Donelson[2] last year advising him to offer terms. He thinks Lord Lyons discreet and blameless so far. He is not afraid of hostilities with England and considers that cry a delusion. He paid four visits to the South raising funds by lecture for the purchase of the Mt. Vernon Estate – $200,000 being the sum required and $74,000 what he got personally.

We went to the Latin School and heard a salvete oration. There was one mulatto in the school. Leslie Stephen made a speech and his simple assertion of Northern sentiments was received with rapturous applause. Dr. Holmes to dinner, a little perky man – talked his own books a good deal. William Everett was quite violent about the unkindness of English opinion and said it was torture being in England the first year of the War.

Strolled after dinner with Leslie Stephen in the Common. Went on to 44 Newton Street to call on Mr. Strong who received me cordially. Captain John Marstern, inspector of lighthouses, fifty years in the Navy, was there. Mrs. Wise, Mr. Everett's daughter, said he was an old stick and had run his ship the *Minnesota* aground. But he seems to have fought her well when she was saved from the *Merrimac* by the *Monitor*. Lieutenant Worden,[3] who commanded the

2. Fort Donelson: Grant's first important victory, February 6, 1862. From this he gets the name 'unconditional surrender Grant'.

3. Lieutenant Worden was a naval hero of the War and the famous duel between *Merrimac* and *Monitor* was a unique episode in naval warfare. After the Norfolk shipyard fell into their hands the Confederates refloated the frigate *Merrimac* and built an iron-plated superstructure upon the hull. At about the same time the Federal Government started building an armoured turret ship, *Monitor*, in New York. The five Northern warships, of which *Minnesota* was one, lying off the port of Norfolk were wooden ships, powerless against an armoured *Merrimac*. *Monitor* and *Merrimac* were completed almost at the same time. *Monitor*, built to a peculiar design, was barely sea-worthy, and it was largely due to the tenacity of her commander, Lieutenant Worden, that she completed the journey from New York to Hampton Roads on March 8, 1862. On that day *Merrimac* came out of Norfolk with the intention of pulverizing the Northern fleet. She dealt effectively with two of the Northern ships; but when she attacked *Minnesota*, *Monitor* was already in position. There followed the historic fight between *Merrimac* and *Monitor*, two unwieldy dinosaurs battering at each other in single combat. This was the first action ever fought by armoured vessels. Neither ship could sink the other, but *Merrimac* drew off and did not attack the wooden ships again. *Minnesota* and the rest were saved and the Confederacy was robbed of a naval victory which would have been valuable at that stage of the War. Lieutenant Worden, who had shown both gallantry and resourcefulness, was seriously wounded in the engagement.

In May 1862 the Confederates destroyed *Merrimac* when the Army of the Potomac was threatening Norfolk. In the following December *Monitor* foundered at sea with part of her crew.

ORDER OF EXERCISES

AT THE

ANNUAL EXHIBITION

OF THE

Public Latin School,

SATURDAY, JULY 11, 1863,

AT 10 O'CLOCK, A. M.

EXERCISES OF THE GRADUATING CLASS.

SALUTATORY ORATION IN LATIN, . . . Nelson L. Derby

DECLAMATION, ... Matthew R. Clark.

TRANSLATION INTO GREEK, ... James R. Carrét.

TRANSLATION INTO LATIN, . . . George W. Eaton.

DECLAMATION, ... Francis M. Stanwood.

LATIN DIALOGUE, The Weathercock.
  OLD FICKLE, ... Charles H. Mann.
  TRISTRAM FICKLE, ... William R. Ellis.

TRANSLATION INTO LATIN, ... Henry G. Monks.

ENGLISH ESSAY. . . . . Arthur Brooks.

VALEDICTORY IN LATIN, ... James B. Ames.

Extracts from the programme
of an exhibition at the Latin
School, Boston.

[39]

The Draft Riots in New York (from *Harper's Weekly*, July 15, 1863)

Monitor was cured of his wounds by Mrs. Wise. I thought Captain Marstern a very fine old gentleman.

SUNDAY, JULY 12

Boston

Went to two sleepy Unitarian services. After the second service walked with Mr. Edward Everett onto the Common and so home. Mr. Everett discoursed upon what had led to Lincoln's election,[4] sketching the origin of the Republican Party. Seward was the main organizer of it and should have been President; but in the Chicago Convention local feeling ran so high that Lincoln was substituted for him. Lincoln had had the better of Douglas* in his speeches and his national reputation dated from his contest with Douglas for the Senatorship two years previously. Seward knew the South well and did not believe they would be easily subjugated. Mr. Everett greatly regretted the split in the Democratic Party at the election: they should have united under some less violent man than Breckinridge*.

In the evening Mrs. Wise expressed great abhorrence of abolitionism: 'it is too disgusting that we should be supposed to be fighting for these niggers. We are fighting for the Union.'

MONDAY, JULY 13

Boston

I visited the Provost-Marshal's Office. In this ward 400 out of 1,300 is about the proportion drafted. There was a good deal of joking going on in the crowded room. Well for them that they can afford to treat it so lightly, for the Conscription Act is a severe measure. Two sons of Mr. Everett and sons of Mr. Garrison and of Mr. Winthrop* have been caught, as also a young fellow whom I met last night. This, considering how few names I know, is pretty well. No wonder there are riots in New York.[5]

4. Edward Everett kept a diary and in it he describes his day on September 12, 1863, as follows: 'To church all day. Mr. Ellis officiated in the morning and Mr. Tilden in the P.M. Called with Mr. Thompson on Dr. Lothrop but he was not in town. Endeavoured by the way to give Mr. Thompson in reply to his enquiries an idea of our recent political history and why Mr. Lincoln – or rather how, he was elected, it being, however, no easy task to compress the events of years into ten minutes explanation.'

5. The New York riots were ignited by the publication on July 12 of the names of those included in the first enlistment draft. According to estimates at the time 1,000 persons were killed or wounded in the riots. The riots were suppressed after four days by troops returning from the Battle of Gettysburg. Congress had passed the Conscription Act in March 1863 requiring all citizens between twenty and forty-five to be called up by draft – the Act to be implemented by Federal agents.

Mr. Everett gave me this morning his July 4 oration of 1860. He quotes Earl Grey in a Reform debate of April 1860 accusing the Republic as having degenerated owing to universal suffrage; and he points to the fruits produced by universal suffrage in America, in material progress, arts, literature and religion, as the answer to this. I then read Mr. E.'s address of July 4, 1861, at Newport in which he proves his case of right being on the side of the Union to suppress secession.

Called on Mr. Charles Eliot Norton at Cambridge. Little man with moustache and tendency to baldness. An abolitionist propagating his ideas in the form of broadsheets to country newspapers containing articles for them to insert. He says that everywhere the trend is toward radicalism. Mr. Everett's Union Club speech this year did not suit him – he objected to the praise of McLellan* and the absence of abolitionism.

TUESDAY, JULY 14

Boston

Last night a canister shot was fired into the mob in Boston by one Captain Jones who was praised in this morning's papers.

WEDNESDAY, JULY 15

Boston

Harvard Commencement Day. Went to Cambridge with William Everett, met in Library and formed procession at 10.00 a.m. After four hours hearing essays formed new procession to the Hall. We dined. I sat at the President's table with Sibley*, the Librarian, who led the Psalm with unction, Lowell, Stephen, Mr. Everett and Mr. Silsby*. The latter told me he had tried some good letters of introduction in England without success: letters even from Mr. Everett availed nothing. He knew intimately Major Anderson* of Fort Sumter: 'his mind is all but gone'. Lowell is agreeable with a reddish beard and coarse hair parted in the middle. They were all shocked by Stephen's way of speaking about Prince Albert. All were abolitionists. Norton took me home to tea.

[42]

> The anniversary of the Alumni. I took Mr. Thompson as I did yesterday, the walked with me both days in the procession. Dr. Walker delivered an admirable Address. After the address came the dinner in the Hall. Owing &.

> A little weary from the exertions of the two last days. In the morning, at Mr. Charles Hale's request, I wrote out my speech yesterday. He dined with us to meet Mr. Thompson, who left in the P.M., an amiable & intelligent young man, A year before N. at Cambridge. The riot at Newyork, instead of being suppressed, as we had hoped, is raging, it is said, with renewed violence. Whatever it was originally, it is now a war, as, I remark yester-

From Edward Everett's diary, July 16.

FRIDAY, JULY 17

Concord, Massachusetts

Yesterday morning went with Mr. Edward Everett by carriage and street-car to Cambridge. The alumni or old Harvard graduates met in the Library. It was filled with men in black trousers of all ages with black ties. Mr. Everett took me alongside of him in the procession which was marshalled two and two. The elders marched between the files of their juniors, Mr. Everett jocosely remarking 'Well boys, we are having a good time: your turn will come some day.' The president [Dr. Hill] sat in the centre of the church before the altar facing the congregation. Dr. Walker* took the chair in front of him. Mr. Everett and Mr. Quincy Jnr.*, ninety-two years old, sat on the left with me, behind Mr. Everett and Colonel Aspinwall of the class of 1804 who lost his arm in 1812 and was thirty-eight years Consul in London. Dr. Walker discoursed on the duties of the educated classes in politics. He defended the University against those who say that her training does not fit men for politics and cited as an example the English statesmen bred at the Universities who whatever were their faults were 'neither theorists nor pedants'. He ended with an eloquent mention of the forty-four Harvard men killed in the War and a suggestion for their monument and its epitaph.

I was taken by young Appleton (drafted and going) to the Porcellian, a secret club where books and bottles filled the room. The subscription is $200 a year, an immense sum. It has two rooms – takes *Punch, Illustrated London News,* etc.

Procession again to the Dining Hall where I sat next to President Hill. Dr. Holmes made a capital Chairman of the alumni vice Mr. Winthrop who wrote to apologize. President Hill made a poor speech. Mr. Quincy was now assisted in (he has a thigh top broken). He sat in a chair and read his speech which consisted of extracts adverse to slavery from his father's journal in the South. Leslie Stephen spoke well – urged them not to go by *The Times* and *Saturday Review.* My health was proposed by Mr. Everett. Thinking this a possible contingency I had prepared something like the following:

'It has been very interesting for me coming straight from Cambridge, England, to find here an institution so similar and so prosperous. To a certain extent I knew what to expect. For you sent over to us four years ago a living advertisement of your system of education in the person of my friend, Mr. William Everett. His distinguished career amazed us and the trophies which he carried off from us show not only his individual ability but also the soundness of the system under which he was trained.

'Here I should sit down but that I consider no Englishman should address Americans at present without a few words on the state of feeling of the English nation on your great question. I lay great stress on the circumstance that the English are very ignorant of America. We have not, like you, been studying for forty years the great conflict between South and North, between slave states and free states, which has in one form or another been constantly progressing in this country.'

Stephen took the same tack and he mentioned young Everett. I should have mentioned him too; but I was frightened and forgot. The *Daily Advertiser* did *full* justice to my speech. Dr. Holmes then proposed the health of young Everett who lauded his father's classmates. Mr. Richard Henry Dana, District Attorney for Massachusetts, made a good savage anti-riot speech. Dr. Clarke[6] told anecdotes of Gettysburg and prayed for vengeance on New York saying that General Benjamin F. Butler* should be sent there. Mr. Everett's speech was capital. He is a fine orator with a notable voice and manner. Dr. Holmes introduced him 'the scholar, the statesman, the orator – Edward Everett'. Mr. Everett rose and said: 'There is no mistaking a man's name though the description preceding the name be ever so little to be recognized.' He referred to the fall of Port Hudson; and, after alluding to the Harvard men killed in battle, he said: 'Good heavens, Sir, and it is said that our armies are composed of the scum of the earth.'[7]

This morning Mr. Everett had his flag out for the victory of Port Hudson. About these New York riots – Government has been very impolitic. The draft had been deferred too long and will be difficult to carry out fully. Curious how war-like the College of Harvard was yesterday: the sentiment most rapturously applauded was that the New York mob should be swept away and the draft enforced at the point of the bayonet.

Mr. Everett has a bad cough: at parting he was very cordial and kind. Mrs. Wise gave me her husband's card at Washington (Commander H. A.

6. Probably the Revd. J. F. Clarke, an eminent Transcendentalist.
7. Edward Everett's reference to the Unionist armies being composed of 'the scum of the earth' is probably derived from one of W. H. Russell's dispatches to *The Times* from Washington at the time of the Battle of Bull Run (see note page 12).

Edward Everett's speech on this occasion was afterwards included among his published speeches. It begins thus: 'While there is that in the state of the country which makes me almost ready to exclaim with Livius that "we have fallen on days when we can neither bear our vices nor their remedies", while even around us the bitter waters of strife are gushing up, in the midst of that fount of patriotic joy opened upon us by our late glorious victories, every dutiful son of Harvard, who has passed yesterday or today at Cambridge must have felt that it was good to be here. Sure I am that the first care of those gathered together as we now are, at the close of this wicked war, will be to lay the cornerstone of the monument to the sons of Harvard who died for their country.'

An entry in Edward Everett's diary on the same day July 17, 1863, reads: 'A little weary from the exertions of the two last days. In the morning at Mr. Charles Hale's request I wrote out my speech of yesterday. He dined with us to meet Mr. Thompson, who left in the P.M., an amiable and intelligent young man a year before William at Cambridge.'

Wise, United States Navy). William Everett rung my hand affectionately. I don't know whether he likes me or not. I think not. He is very clever, but I think lacking in judgement.

I now go to bed at the Middlesex Hotel, Concord. Shall I send the following letter to the *Daily News*?

> *Wednesday last was Commencement Day at Cambridge University, Mass. One of the formalities observed was the distribution of a list of students who have died in the country's service from the beginning of the Rebellion to April 15, 1863. This list includes forty-four names. Out of these forty-four no less than thirty-seven perished within the last twelve months, more than half the whole number of graduates who died during that period. Now, Sir, I appeal to those reckless writers who have insisted that the Northern armies are the scum of the earth and ask them if this one fact does not prove the contrary. I doubt if any University in any land has ever made a greater sacrifice in proportion to its numbers. Our own Cambridge in a similar cause might do as much, but no one could expect her to do more. If it were understood in England that the educated classes in New England are enthusiastic for the War, many people, who are now content to judge hastily on the great questions at issue between North and South, would examine them more deeply in order to see why it is that grave and thoughtful men cheerfully sacrifice their sons.*

SATURDAY, JULY 18

Concord

Made my call on Mr. Hawthorne. He desired remembrances to Henry Bright. The son, Julian, was at dinner and took me for a rainy walk afterwards by the old Manse and across the Concord river. Mr. Hawthorne talked for some time of politics. He is in despair about the war and the country and he is a copperhead of copperheads. Mr. Hawthorne has all the prejudices about the negroes — 'they smell, their intellects are inferior', etc., etc. He gave me pleasant California hock, bad claret and bad beer. He showed me his 'cloister', with the track made by himself pacing it, on the top of a rise beyond the house. He took me to Mr. Emerson's, who is a tallish Yankee-looking man with short whiskers, long black, very scanty hair and large brow. He was busy about an address to a school and could not come to dine with us. He said that the English do not venerate their ancient buildings.

Nathaniel Hawthorne (from a photo in the Boston Athenaeum).

Wendell Phillips (bust by John Adams Jackson in the Boston Athenaeum).

SUNDAY, JULY 19

Keene, New Hampshire

Sent off my letter, revised, to the *Daily News* this morning. I am staying at the house of Mr. and Mrs. White who are charming people. He is a Unitarian Minister and a strong abolitionist. It has been raining hard all day. Read Tocqueville[8] with great benefit. I must record some of my reading. 'Causes of the Civil War in America' by John Lothrop Motley, reprinted from his articles in the London *Times* 1861, is a real textbook for Unionists. A Confederacy had been tried from 1781 to 1787 and found to mean, after peace was obtained (1783), anarchy. The Continental Congress was a Diet of envoys from sovereign States. The Constitution was ordained and established over the States by a power superior to the States — by the people of the whole land acting in their aggregate capacity through conventions of Delegates expressly chosen for the purpose within each State independently of the State governments.

I have glanced over Mr. Sumner's speech delivered in May 1856 in the Senate. It is an accusation of Butler of South Carolina and Douglas of Illinois for their part in breaking the Missouri compromise.[9] Douglas in reply asks

8. *Democracy in America* by Alexis de Tocqueville, 1835.

9. The Kansas–Nebraska Act of 1854 made a breach in the Missouri Compromise of 1820 and resulted in a minor civil war in the State of Kansas between those for and those against slavery. In May 1856 Charles Sumner made a violent attack in the Senate on those responsible for 'the crime against Kansas' naming Senator Andrew Butler of South Carolina, whose nephew entered the Senate two days later and assaulted Sumner with a heavy stick, seriously injuring him, to the delight of a number of Southern Senators.

Contemporary print depicting assault on Senator Sumner.

[47]

Sumner if he wants to provoke 'some of us to kick him as we would a dog in the street'. Mason speaks of the abolitionists as 'persons whose presence is a dishonour and the touch of whose hands is a disgrace and whom he cannot acknowledge as possessing manhood in any form'.

WEDNESDAY, JULY 22

Keene

Just come in from four mile walk up to Beaver's Brook with Mr. White. Talked of schools and abolition. Mrs. White told me this morning about Mr. White's nephews, the Dwights — one was killed at Antietam,[10] one by guerillas after surrendering at New Orleans, one (a general) desperately wounded at Williamsport, one (a lieutenant) still untouched and one now joining the army. The story of her brothers is curious — one is a colonel in Missouri, one a major for the Union, one was Adjutant-General for the late Government in Missouri, which went Secession, and is now in the Secessionist army and the fourth is at Mobile in the service of the South. Mrs. W. said this haunted her at first, but now she is used to the idea of having two brothers on the Secessionist side.

THURSDAY, JULY 23

Letter to sister Meggie

Keene, New Hampshire

Your and Mamma's letters came today. I answer yours at once. Keep the letter that I may insert it in my notebook on my return.

I have been located with Mr. and Mrs. White since Sunday and leave them on Saturday next. I had a letter from Boston to a certain Mrs. Mary Dinsmore living here who is one of the belles of the place. She got up this week a picnic embracing the elite of Keene society to go up Monadnock, a mountain some twelve miles off. About thirty went, mainly young ladies, for whom this place is famous. The main vehicle was a huge waggon holding fifteen on five cross seats and two on a high box with the

10. The Battle of Antietam in Maryland was fought in September 1862 by the Army of the Potomac against Lee's army which it outnumbered by two to one: casualties on both sides were heavy and the battle was in fact indecisive; but Lee drew off and Antietam counted as a Federal victory.

driver. It had 'The Experiment' in large letters on it, takes four horses, and is very imposing when full. We set off at 8.00 a.m., the ladies, of whom only younger ones went, being dressed most of them in a sort of sensible costume – no crinoline and dresses down to their ankles. Among the youths were two just come back from the armies. 'The Experiment' put us down at the Halfway House, a third way up the mountain. Thence those who were going up set off, the rest staying to get dinner ready. It took an hour and a half to get up with considerable resting, assisting of young ladies, water drinking, etc. by the way. The view from the top is over an undulating farm-covered country. The young ladies are very 'bright', not at all forward but very independent. We had a splendid feast in a shady place with lots of ice and other luxuries and set off home by a different route about 4.00 p.m. Coming home we had no end of singing, especially 'John Brown's Body'. It amuses me to find the girls here well up in Trollope, Tennyson, etc. singing just the same songs as we do – 'Oft in the Stilly Night', 'Auld Lang Syne', etc., etc. They have been working two days a week for the last two years for the army. They are a wonderful average of girls who can talk to you about novels, poetry and politics. It would amuse you to see me playing euchre with three young ladies. They have a surprising number of concoctions from corn here – buckwheat cakes, corn cakes, Sally Lunns, griddle cakes and waffles, all delicacies to which I have been introduced.

I have been a fortnight today in America and have spent only two dollars as yet at hotels; but on Saturday I shall be on the world again. It will be pain and grief to me to leave this haven of repose where I have a charming cool room opening on the garden and a hot bath of a peculiar species of shape and a general smell of lavender.

I am curious to hear what effect the news from here of Union victories has in England. I asked Sam to send me papers – the Spectator every Saturday and The Times and Daily News.

Saturday evening (July 25 at Bethlehem Street). I left Keene this morning and have alighted by the blessing of heaven at a place called Bethlehem Street, a very

Sketch by Yates Thompson of the picnic on Mount Monadnock, New Hampshire.

small village in the *White Mountains. I stopped here quite by chance about dark owing to terrific rain which made the top of the coach unpleasant, and I find a charming little house with fresh trout and honey for supper. I bade an affecting farewell to Mrs. White this morning. Her husband left home yesterday for Salem where he is to preach on Sunday. I made a sketch of their Rockaway or small carriage, in which I was taken some lovely drives.*

Monday (July 27 at Profile House, N.H.). This is a large hotel and so full that on getting here last night I was unable to get a room and slept in the drawing room. I drove over from Bethlehem Street yesterday afternoon over a deep-rutted road between thick trees all the way except where there was an occasional farm, which means here a white wooden house with a verandah and, on a Sunday afternoon, a Yankee in a rocking chair reading under its shade. I am a good deal amazed by the Yankees at the hotel. The dressing is very extensive among the ladies. The New Yorkers seem to predominate, a horrid set of snobs — leastways many of them are.

FRIDAY, JULY 24

Letter to William Everett

Keene, New Hampshire

I am leaving Keene tomorrow and write to tell you that I have had a real good time here. I have been staying since Sunday with Mr. White under whose auspices

Mr. White's Rockaway sketched by Yates Thompson at Monadnock, near Keene, New Hampshire.

I have seen Keene to great advantage. Please tell this to Mr. Charles Hale[11] as it is to him that I owe having been here and making Mr. and Mrs. White's acquaintance. His friend Mrs. Dinsmore has also been most hospitable and invited me yesterday to a picnic up Monadnock in the course of which I saw the elite of Keene. It is very entertaining to me having a peep into the interior of New England. Everything is new to me from the hot bath to the Rockaway.

I have been much impressed by finding a quiet country parson so immersed in warlike interest as Mr. White is. He could not be more enthusiastic if they were invading New Hampshire. I am very curious to see The Times *on the taking of Vicksburg. They will be at a loss whether to retreat from their opinions absolutely, acquiesce in the possibility of Union victory and recommend moderation, an amnesty, etc. or to lay stress on the riots and effect their change of sentiments more leisurely.*

I hope your party is flourishing and that Mr. Everett has got rid of his cough. I shall always remember the time I spent in his house with great pleasure.

TUESDAY, JULY 28

White Mountain House ('Brabrook's'), New Hampshire

Met a man at Profile House, honest, Scottish descent, keen for the draft. Told me he had a brother at Antietam last year — only enlisted in August and went into battle in September quite undrilled, wounded in leg and now has a hospital post.

Pleasant forest drive today to 'Brabrook's' with a Dr. Storrs of Brooklyn and daughter Harriet. Read all afternoon Tocqueville and Olmsted, the latter on his journey from Richmond to Petersburg, Norfolk, Wilmington and Charleston.

WEDNESDAY, JULY 29

Letter to brother Rodie

White Mountain House ('Brabrook's')

I have been up a mountain today — the highest of the White Mountains, Mt. Washington. The top is a good twelve miles off. I took a horse for twelve dollars. I

11. Charles Hale was a nephew of Edward Everett and a journalist on a Boston newspaper.

started with a one-eyed guide, he having gone into the army and lost his eye by the explosion of one of his own caps while being drilled. The top of the mountain was a failure owing to cloud. These mountains are too fashionable and full for my taste. I shall go into Canada and try for some salmon before the fall. I am busy reading Olmsted's Cotton Kingdom. *If anybody wants some data to judge the American question by, no better book can be found. Henry Bright ought to get it: tell him to read it and see what a charming state of society his Southern friends wish to perpetuate.*

The danger for the North is division. Many people here think that the New York riots were intended to begin a civil war in the North. The copperheads, so called from the name of the most disgusting sort of snake in America, are the old pro-South Democrats who have controlled the Union government for the last forty years almost without exception. This is the party which established the bad character of the Union government and pushed forward slavery. Now they are dying to get into power again and are supposed to have winked at the New York riots with the object of embarrassing the Government. The riots have done them harm and strengthened the Government.

FRIDAY, JULY 31

Gorham, New Hampshire

My journey yesterday went off very well. Mr. Brabrook drove over five of us including Dr. Storrs and his daughter in a covered waggon. There was with us a Mr. George Walker of Springfield, Mass., a State politician, has been in the Massachusetts Senate and is now employed by the State government as inspector of banks. He considers the Union can stand a debt of 2,000 million dollars without anybody being much incommoded. At present, he says, the individual prosperity in the North is greater than it ever was. All the private companies such as banks, manufacturing, railways, etc. are doing wonderfully well and there has been no difficulty in collecting taxes. He struck me as a thoughtful man and he knows English history far better than I do. He says the financial authorities in the U.S. look almost entirely to English precedent for their measures. When the war ends he expects a crash owing to stoppage of government orders and disbanding of the armies; but he thinks it will be mitigated by the great power of the country to absorb labour. Certainly New Hampshire could absorb more labour now: Mr. Brabrook informed me that he can only get haymakers at two dollars a day – fine weather – which means they won't work in the wet and have to be paid all the same.

Canadian Interlude

EDITOR'S NOTE

THE HOT MONTH of August was spent in Canada. After breakfast at Gorham, New Hampshire, on Saturday, August 1, our traveller parted affectionately with his friend Dr. Storrs, whom he met in the White Mountains, promising to visit him in due course at Brooklyn. He went by train to Sherbrooke, Canada, passing through Customs at Island Pond and finishing Olmsted's *Cotton Kingdom* on the journey. It was not until August 29 that he returned to the United States from Niagara Falls to Syracuse. In Canada he picked up friends as he went, presenting his letters of introduction and recording the day's doings and conversations in his journal. But the August excursion to Canada is not strictly relevant to our theme, which is the American Civil War and a young Englishman's observations thereon. In Canada much of his journal is concerned with fishing trips and scenery. He travelled from Sherbrooke to Montreal with 'Mr. Galt, finance minister in the previous Canadian cabinet, a hale, big-mouthed, scanty-haired, genial man', who arranged some fishing for him and told him how rapidly the French Canadians were increasing and how the farmers in the Sherbrooke area could not sell their produce to the United States, their normal market, because of depreciation of the U.S. currency. He went to Toronto, Ottawa and Quebec and spent the final week at Cataract House, Niagara Falls, which he found 'most enchanting' and 'the rush of water refreshing'. A dinner party was given for him in Quebec by the Canadian Prime Minister, Stanfield Macdonald ('a capital story teller'), on August 17, where the talk was almost entirely about Canadian politics.

He read some English newspapers including an account of an 'American debate' in the House of Commons in which Mr. Gladstone still expressed 'his firm disbelief in any possible reconstitution of the Union'. He found Canada very hot in August and suffered from the mosquitoes. The following extracts from a letter to his father written from Cornwall on August 7, 1863, give an impression of the journey.

FRIDAY, AUGUST 7

Letter to father

Cornwall, Canada West

My last letter was to Rodie from the White Mountains. I left Gorham, N.H., on Friday, July 31. Since then I have spent three days at Sherbrooke, Canada East, two at Montreal, and since Wednesday have been here, staying with a Harrow friend of mine named Holmes, who emigrated on account of a mésalliance, and is living here at Cornwall, studying law with one Stanfield Macdonald, at present Prime Minister of Canada.

It was so hot at Montreal that I came on here by train on Wednesday. I found Holmes very glad to see me. He is living at present in Mr. Macdonald's house. That gentleman is at Quebec where Parliament opens on Thursday. I shall go and see something of it.

I have been employing myself a good deal since I left Boston in reading books on America. Amongst others I lately finished Mr. Spence's book on the Union which was so much praised by The Times. *He too seems to be under the supreme error of believing that the South would of itself abolish slavery, whereas its leading politicians have all declared the contrary. As to Gettysburg, Lee was bloodily repulsed and that was all. The crisis of the War to my mind is on the Mississippi and there the North has never looked back since the War began.*

Sketch by Yates Thompson of the River St. Lawrence, near Cornwall, Canada.

SUNDAY, AUGUST 9

The Canadians I have seen are almost all Southerners. I read yesterday Lord Palmerston's speech on July 23 in answer to Cobden about the shipbuilding. He seems to me to make too much of the difficulty there is in distinguishing between a ship intended for commerce and one meant for war. What will he say to the iron-clads which I saw in Mr. Laird's yard before I left Liverpool? I think the North will be fools if they don't make a great effort to have those stopped even if they have to threaten war. I hope that we should not fight on such a question. I am glad to see the Confederate loan in a bad way. No wonder people are frightened. For besides Lee's army I don't see what else formidable the South have left, and I think his army must be very much less formidable than it was when Jackson* was alive.

Holmes is giving me letters to Mr. Macdonald and others at Quebec and I expect some entertainment there as Mr. Macdonald has to meet a new parliament and he is not certain of a majority. There is great antagonism just now between Upper and Lower Canada on the question of representation by population. It reads very like the late quarrel in the United States.[12] Upper Canada has increased in population till, if representation by proportion is carried, they will have a clear majority. The lower

Yates Thompson stayed at Cataract House during his visit to the Niagara Falls; the menu and guest list (including Yates Thompson) are reproduced overleaf.

12. This refers to the arrangement in the United States, dating from 1787, under which, in assessing the number of Representatives sent by each State to Congress on a basis of population, five slaves were counted as three white men, although slaves had no vote. This was a Northern grievance.

TABLE D'HOTE.

THURSDAY, AUGUST 27, 1863.

Soup.
Vegetable.

Fish.
Baked White Fish, Port Wine Sauce.
Boiled Salmon Trout, Egg Sauce.

Roast.
Ribs of Beef,	Lamb, Mint Sauce,	Chicken, Brown Sauce,
Veal, Brown Sauce,	Stuffed Pig,	Loin Mutton, Brown Sauce.

Side Dishes.
Brisket of Lamb, Broiled, Tomato Sauce,
Veal Cutlet, Fried with Crumbs,
Saute of Kidney, Port Wine Sauce,
Prairie Chicken with Currant Jelly,
Baked Macaroni and Cheese,
Fillet of Fowl, Spanish Sauce,
Escaloped Tomatoes, Baked,
Lambs Heart, Olive Sauce.

Boiled.
Leg of Mutton, Caper Sauce,	Chicken Egg Sauce,	Sugar Cured Ham
Corned Beef,		Buffalo Tongue.

Vegetables.
Potatoes,	Cabbage,		String Beans,
Potatoes—Boiled, Baked and Mashed,		Beets,	Stewed Tomatoes,
Onions,	Squash,	Green Corn,	Rice,
Carrots,	Turnips,	Succotash,	Hominy,

Relishes.
French Mustard,	Cucmbers,	
Olives,	Lettuce.	
Tomatoes		

Sauces.
Worcester,	John Bull
Harvey,	Sultana.
Anchovy,	

Puddings.
Rice,
Custard,
Bread,

Pies.
Apple,
Florance Cream
Berry.

Dessert.
Blancmange,	Lemon Ice Cream,	Peaches,	Almonds,
Jelly,	Charlotte de Russe,		Raisins,
Sponge Cake,	Ripe Apples,	Pears,	White Cake.

Guests having Friends to Dine, will give Notice at the Office.

BREAKFAST .... 7 TO 10
DINNER .... 2 P. M
TEA .... 7 P. M

Pool & Sleeper, Printers, Gazette Office.

WINE LIST.

MADEIRA.

Lewis _____ $3.00
Reserve _____ 3.00
Newton, Gordon & Murdock ____ 4.00
South Side _____ 4.00

SHERRY.

Diaz _____ $2.00
Pemartin _____ 2.50
Sierra _____ 2.50
Yriarte _____ 3.00
Duff Gordon _____ 3.50
Romano _____ 3.50

PORT.

Graham _____ $2.00
Harmony _____ 2.00
London _____ 3.00
Queen's _____ 3.00
Barmeister _____ 4.00

HOCK.

Native _____ $2.00
Rudesheimer _____ 2.50
Macobronner _____ 3.00
Hockheimer _____ 3.00
Liebfranmilch _____ 3.00
Rheinwein _____ 3.50
Sparkling Hockheimer, Henkell & Co. _ 3.50
Johannesberger, yellow seal ___ 4.00

BURGUNDY.

Chambertin _____ $3.50
Romance _____ 4.00
Clos de Veugeot _____ 5.00

Ale, Pints _____ 0.40
do   Quarts _____ 0.75

CHAMPAGNE.

Medal qts. _____ $2.00
Schreider _____ 3.00
  Pints do _____ 2.00
Mumm's Cabinet _____ 3.50
  Pints do _____ 2.00
Napoleon. (Barsalou) Creme de Bouzy
  very fine _____ 3.50
  Pints do _____ 2.00
Heidsieck, [Piper & Co.] _____ 3.00
  Pints do _____ 2.00
Moet & Chandon, green seal, __ 4.00
  Pints, Do, _____ 2.50

CLARET.

St Julien Medoc _____ $1.25
  Pints do _____ 0.75
Blanquefort _____ 2.00
Margaux _____ 2.00
Grand vin de Leoville _____ 2.50
Chateau Lafitte _____ 2.50
Washington Morton _____ 4.00
Chauteau Margaux, [W. Morton.] _ 4.00

SAUTERNE.

Haute Sauterne _____ $2.50
Chablis _____ 2.50

Porter, pints _____ 0.40
do Quarts _____ 0.75

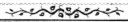 EACH WAITER IS PROVIDED WITH WINE CARDS AND PENCIL.

CATARACT HOUSE
NIAGARA FALLS.

WHITNEY, JERAULD & CO.
PROPRIETORS.

LIST OF ARRIVALS, AUGUST 26, 1863

R G Smith, Jr Brooklyn
Mr Archer, London. C W
Capt W H Pick, w & d, Flushing
Thos L Barret & son, Louisville
A Magin, Brooklyn
W H Purnell & w, Baltimore
S Brady, Detroit
Thos Yocum & w, Philadelphia
Miss A Hamilton   do
S G Smith   do
Thos Lu Brent, U S N
O C Johnson & w, Kendall, N Y
Mrs S L Bonha   Peru, Ia
Thos Ryerson, & son, Newton
W H Clark & w, Earlson
Mr M Hudrickson, N Y
G C Fairman, Milwaukee
Peter J Coughlin, St Louis
E J Howe & 2 l, Lockport
H Rogers, N Adams
G B Brand, Rochester
H A Smith & w, North Adams
C F Patten, Enfie d, N H
C C Barrett, Mass
F H Goodspeed & w, Mass
Mrs P P Gould   do
J Lockett & sis, Brooklyn
Chas Lockett & sis, do
Mr McLarier, Hamilton, C W
Gilman Riddle, N H
Mrs Bell French do
Mrs Abbott   do
Miss Bunton   do
Miss Fuller   do
Mrs Tatom   do
Thos Sargent & d do
J C Clark & w, Delaware
B Reybold & w   do
W Reybold & w   do
Miss A Cleaver   do
Miss E Cleaver   do
Miss J Cleaver   do
G Von Grabow, Washington, D C
F Wheatley & d, Georgetown
Mrs McKean & friend, Albany

Elihu Day & w, Newark, N J
Miss J L Day   do
Miss O F Day   do
J B Austin & w, Philadelphia
J E Austin   do
J Bell Austin   do
Mrs H Gray, Elmira
S C Gray   do
W H Blodgett, Boston
A Rumsey, w & d,
Miss Dana
H Parmalee & w. Buffalo
J D Vernulye & w, Newark N J
Miss Ann Vernulye   do
Ira Brockett & w. Galway, N Y
Miss G Darrogh, Sharon, Pa
Miss Adda H Linton, Rochester, Pa
Miss Lydia M Reno   do
Miss A Reno   do
T P Wilson, U S N
A J Mancy, Freeport; Ill
W Auberry & 2 d, Cincinnati
H Y Thompson, England
Chas S Hunt, St Louis
Theo Hunt   do
C H Turner   do
W M Turner   do
Chas Maffit   do
D F Raymond & w, Cincinnati
A C A Rosing & w   do
C B Church & svt, Memphis
Miss M L Church   do
Miss Julia F azier do
Miss Anna Carrell   do
J J Beardsley & w,
T H Handbury, West Point
Peter R Costelyou, Hemp tead
Miss Lottie Costelyen do
W C Hasbroack, w & son Newburg
Judie P Allen, New Haven
Miss Rutledge   do
Beverly Allen   do
Geo G Coffin, Jr, New York
Miss Mary E Coffin do

G Y Wa d, Ky
W F Barrett, w & d, Louisville
H C Wood   do
L M Guthrie   do
A P Winslow, Cleveland
Edward Faxon, N Y
Robt Robinson do
Richard Ashbridge, Chester Co, Pa
Wm Ashbridge   do
Miss Lenn Cruft, Terre Haute
Miss Fann e L Croft do
Miss F D Spencer, Erie, Pa
W Spenc r   do
W M Blackburn
W Dunn & w, Cincinnati
Miss Wone s   do
Miss Hattie W Brown, Watervill
Mr & Mrs Snepard, Buffalo
Dr E Schilling. N Y
L A Penfield & w, N Y
Dr Wood, U S A
Isaac C Jackson & wife Plymouth
G B Door, Lenox
F F Door   do
J Selever & w, E'mira
Miss Mary Selover do
Mrs Lockwood & fam, N Y
Arthur Laurence, Boston
Geo B Keith & w, New York
D M Turner & w   do
Miss Turner   do
Miss Baldwin   do
S W Baldwin   do
P A Gray & w   do
Miss Lee   do
Miss Gray   do
D Jone , w & c, Boston
Mrs Gilmore & c do
Mrs Rockwell & c do
Mr & Mrs W B Thomas, Phil a
Misses Thomas   do
Mr & Mrs Nathan Brook do
Benj Gethens   do

DEPARTURE OF CARS.

TRAINS LEAVE FOR THE EAST—Express, 4:30 A. M.; Steamboat Express, 7:00 A. M., Mail 2:00 P. M., connecting at Charlotte with the American Line of Steamers for Montreal; Express, 5:10 and 6:15 P. M.

FOR BUFFALO—8:00 A. M., 1:10 and 6:20 P. M.

FOR LEWISTON—9:10 A. M. and Charlotte [Genesee River] at 2 P. M. to connect with American Express Steamer for Montreal,

FOR THE WEST, Via the Great Western (Canada) Railway—9:10 A. M. 7:30 P. M

HOP THIS EVENING.

Canadians, mainly French and conservatives, threaten separation if this comes to pass.

If the French do go to war with Russia on Poland I don't see where it will end. I have no doubt that you are very despondent on the subject.

SATURDAY, AUGUST 29

Syracuse, New York State
(pronounced 'Sirrah-kewse' by the inhabitants)

I left the Niagara Falls at 5.10 a.m. Before leaving I crossed by the ferry (20 cts) to Canada, rowed across by a man with whom I afterwards walked up to the site of the battle of Lundy's Lane.[13] He was from New Jersey which he left early in the War and now lives in Canada. Many did likewise. At present times are excellent in the States and will remain so while the War lasts – to prove this my friend cited the prosperity of England in the time of the French war. He had hawked crockery about the South.

'The planters are real gentlemen. Why, Sir, when he knew I was come, a planter would send down his carriage to take me to church. No one would do that in the North or in Canada.'

The Yankees are setting up manufacturing enterprises in many Canadian towns, especially in Toronto.

In the train I sat next to Col. J. Wood of Munfordville, Kentucky. He told me that the reason for Kentuckian neutrality when the War began was that the Government and the Legislature were on different sides and nothing could be done till a new election. The pro-Southern Legislature was then displaced and the State at once declared for the Union. 'Kentucky, Sir, believe me is overwhelmingly for the Union.' 'I suppose Morgan* did considerable damage in your neighbourhood?' 'I will tell you exactly what damage he did. He took some hundreds of horses and burnt some houses. I can tell you some facts which not many men seem to be aware of. Morgan's entering Ohio was in this way. He crossed first from Tennessee into Kentucky. That was before any of the Federal successes – Vicksburg, Port Hudson, Gettysburg. His cavalry force was to have been followed by an army of infantry and the invasion of Kentucky was meant to be permanent. Owing to Confederate disasters the infantry did not follow Morgan and he was recalled. The message however did not reach him in time and he was cut off near the Ohio river by Hobson. He was driven to cross

13. Lundy's Lane was the scene of an indecisive battle fought on July 25, 1814, between two small British and American armies.

[59]

the river to save himself.' 'And what is the state of things with the slaves in Kentucky now?' 'Well, Sir, wherever the armies come the slaves cannot be kept together without great difficulty, but in the main things remain as they were. I tell you, Sir, I own slaves myself and if I saw how to get rid of them I would jump at it. Slavery is not profitable.' His friend sitting with us then put in that it was well known that Colonel Wood was the greatest slave on his own plantations. I mentioned having met an Ohio officer at Niagara who had been wounded at Murfreesboro.[14] Colonel Wood said : 'I had a son wounded in that battle'. He got out at Lockport with his friend of the name of Thompson, inviting me to come and see him if I ever came to Munfordville.

I got to bed last night at the Globe Inn, Syracuse, N.Y. This morning I called on the Revd. Sam J. May,* Unitarian Minister — a short man with a keen

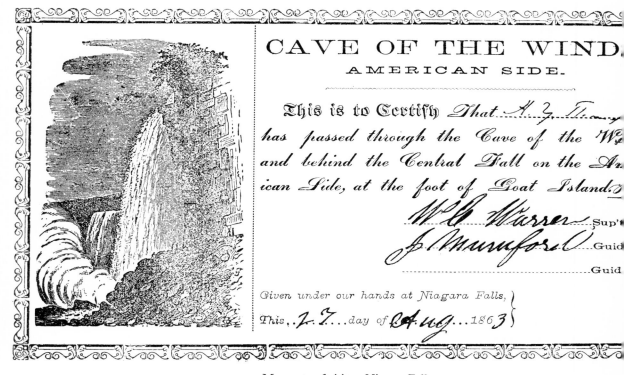

Memento of visit to Niagara Falls.

14. At Murfreesboro, Tennessee, in the last days of December 1862, a desperate battle was fought on frozen ground by General Rosecrans commanding the Army of the Cumberland against General Bragg. The Federals lost 13,000 men killed and wounded and the Confederates 10,000, but the Confederates withdrew from the field and retreated southwards.

eye and grey fringe of hair. The ladies here are working one day a week for the Sanitary Commission. Professor White came in and had tea with us. He talked of the White Mountains, where he made an excursion after graduating with several of his class-mates including Mr. Ware* author of Zenobia, of Niagara and of Mr. Everett.

I bought for fifteen cents 'A word from the North West States to Russell.'[15] It is I think by Professor White whom I met this morning: the anti-English feeling here now is not the same as in the old war – this is a new current of ill feeling caused by the anti-Northern tone of England after secession was mooted.

SUNDAY, AUGUST 30

Syracuse

An interesting day. I read T. M. Thayer's *Pioneer Boy* being a life of Abe Lincoln in his early days. It is a first-rate boy's book and interesting anyway. I went into a Scotch Presbyterian Church on the roadside. A tall young man, Johnstone by name, was preaching on 'Blessed are the peacemakers'. He quoted Wellington as an example of duty. He referred to the persecution of the Scotch Covenanters and the French Protestants. He expounded the abolitionist theory of the War. I walked on and sat on a bridge and finished reading the book on Abe Lincoln.

Mrs. May is an Anglomaniac and says she is almost an Englishwoman. She admires Addison so much that she has a picture of him in her room.

Mr. May talked to me about American politics. He gave me the story of Mr. Everett's non-re-election as Governor of Massachusetts, through 5,000 voters abstaining. Mr. E. in his message had proposed that abolitionists should be prosecuted. He failed to be re-elected by one vote.

MONDAY, AUGUST 31

Syracuse

Mr. Alfred Wilkinson, son-in-law of Mr. May, took me for a drive in his buggy round Syracuse. Manufactories springing up right and left. Prosperity never so great. Wilkinson said feeling in the west about the War was just as strong as in the east. He was very bitter against France about Mexico: he gets

15. This probably refers to William Howard Russell, Washington correspondent of the London *Times*.

fonder of Lincoln every day. We saw a great crowd to receive the 10th New York regiment back from Port Hudson – scenes of wild enthusiasm. With Mrs. Banks – a motherly woman, she told one of the soldiers how glad she was to see him back alive. I talked with a regular Yankee who said feeling was very strong against England on account of the privateers – but he did not believe this could be the act of 'the people of England'.

TUESDAY, SEPTEMBER 1

Letter to mother

Albany

At Syracuse Mr. Samuel J. May, a noted abolitionist, treated me very well and told me a great deal that was interesting. He had been involved in the 'underground railway' and says that they used to pass about two hundred escaped slaves every year through Syracuse on the way to Canada. These people are all as keen about the war as you can imagine, and the more educated and quiet looking they are the keener they seem to be. At Niagara I met an old gentleman from Kentucky – the perfect picture of old-fashioned America, immensely tall with a black felt hat, scrupulously dressed in black and carrying a splendid gold-headed cane. He turned out to be Colonel J. Wood who lives near the Mammoth Cave in Kentucky. He told me that he was a slave-owner but was for the Union for all that, as was an immense majority in Kentucky. Three battles were fought close to his house and one of his sons was wounded; but the country is settled now. It astonishes me how much curiosity there is everywhere about the views of the English on the war. Some profess great disgust at the support we have given to the rebellion. But most expect that our opinion will come over to their side in time and this is what I expect. Mr. Lincoln is by no means such a fool as we have been taught to believe. He will leave behind him a great reputation. At Niagara I made an alliance with an officer from Rosecrans's army. He was wounded at Murfreesboro and goes about limping. His admiration for Rosecrans* is extreme. Many think that it is he who will decide the war if his present advance proves successful.

THURSDAY, SEPTEMBER 3

Boston

Went to Springfield to visit Mr. G. Walker whom I met in New Hampshire. I walked up Main Street and was then directed to turn uphill to my left which I did into a shady street with houses on one side and terrace down to Main Street on the other. Mr. Walker lives in the third house – brick painted brown, square with verandahs on both sides. I had just pulled the bell when Mr. W. arrived from his father-in-law's house, whence he had probably seen me, with 'I am glad to see you Mr. Thompson'. We went in and talked about my journey since we parted at Jefferson, N.H. A couple of children were playing in the library, a nice room looking onto the garden. We talked a good deal. Then Captain, a big horse, came round with the buggy and we drove to the Government establishment. The Enfield machinery was imitated at Springfield, several workmen going hence to Enfield. We visited the storehouse where Mr. Gates showed us samples of European rifles, especially one of huge bore made in Germany. He considered the Enfield bayonet clumsy, too heavy for its length and liable to bend the barrel. He had one such rifle from Antietam broken in two places. 850 rifles a day are turned out here on the average. In action the destruction of arms is immense.

I had much conversation with Mr. Walker. These Yankees have very varied lives. He began with law, then took to financial reading and business. We discussed Mr. Everett. Walker said he was 'emasculated by over-refinement of mind': the bond between him and his constituents broke. Mr. Everett's apology for his speech of indignation after Sumner's assault[16] was droll and has become a byword. 'He had just taken an anodyne and was under its influence.' No chance of his ever being in office again.

About John Brown* – Mr. Walker had actually had him in that room. He came in to get supplies, nominally for relief in Kansas ; but, as Mr. Walker said, undoubtedly for his Virginian expedition.

I got back to Boston late last night and I am staying at Revere House this time. The Everetts asked me again, but they have a house full and I declined. Found a copy of *Daily News* with my letter in it. Got letter from Trevelyan* [Sir George Otto]. Wrote to Papa on his political argument – unanimity of South – and also to Mamma on hers – the right to secede. My friend William Everett is quite developing as an orator himself. He has addressed three meetings already and will I think become noted in the same line as his father. The public spirit of young Americans is very intense. The stakes are enormous, but there is so much energy and faith in these people that I believe they can in their present temper carry almost anything. Mr. Lincoln is getting more trusted every day. Went to the Athenaeum Picture Gallery – bust of Wendell Phillips with clearcut mouth and refined air. At the Everetts at 2.30 p.m. Edward Everett Hale* came to dinner : talk on books, too learned for me. Hale walked with me to the depot of the Sanitary Commission. A young lady (Miss Appleton) was keeping the

16. Assault on Senator Sumner (see note 9, page 47).

[63]

information contained in them.

Mr. Thompson & Edward Hale dined with
us today. Thompson reports a violent controversy
going on between the Upper & lower Provinces of
Canada. Very virulent language used in debate,
such as calling an Opponent "Boudreau".

_____ to _____

publication in his paper this P. M.
Mr. Thompson of Liverpool returned from
his Canadian tour, but did not come to
my house to stay. Read a good deal in in of
Olmsted's books.

From Edward Everett's diary, September 3 and 4.

books most neatly. This is entirely done by volunteer young ladies who seem to
have inherited the skill of their mercantile fathers.

FRIDAY, SEPTEMBER 4

Letter to father

Revere House, Boston

*I have been very much struck by the well-to-do appearance of free negroes in
these north-eastern states. I never saw a set of people bearing more marks of quiet*

industry, many of whom are escaped slaves. It did, indeed, look at one time as if the Rebellion might establish itself as a Revolution, but the North by gigantic sacrifices has put things into a different state now and I believe you may have Jefferson Davis as a refugee in Liverpool before long. Have you seen Mr. Lincoln's letter to the Union meeting in Illinois.[17] He is acting very honestly and boldly and he will leave a great name in history, a fame analogous to that of Pitt. I do not apprehend any more riots in New York. The draft has been carried through there. I am thinking of staying here for a week and then going to New York. I passed a day in Springfield on my way from Albany. It is the place where the Government's small arms are made.

FRIDAY, SEPTEMBER 4

Boston

Wrote another letter to *Daily News* which took me most of the day. Found Mr. Everett and W. Everett at 7.00 p.m.

SATURDAY, SEPTEMBER 5

Boston

Out after breakfast went to call on Wendell Phillips. I walked upstairs by the direction of a maid-servant. It was a mean looking room where Mr. Phillips sat talking with a regular westerner who spoke of his district in Illinois and hoped to see Mr. Phillips there. Mr. Phillips said he thought he could not go west this year. He had too much to do in the east. The man went away with a copy of Mr. Phillips's speeches. Mr. Phillips is tall and thin, very pale and I should say in weak health. He said that Tocqueville understood this country better than any other man. He spoke of its intolerance. 'If a man professes certain sentiments no one will employ him as a lawyer: Society enslaves him into submission.' And as for the press – the *Daily Advertiser* had an article on him: he asked to answer it in their pages: they said no. He could notice a great change in his personal treatment recently. Formerly he could not walk the streets without

17. A mass meeting of 'Union Men' convened in Illinois to discuss the policy of the Government. Lincoln sent a letter to be read out at the meeting in which he made it plain in the simplest language the impossibility of a negotiated peace in the light of the promise made to the negroes in his Emancipation Proclamation – 'the promise being made must be kept'.

hearing some man say, for him to hear, that he ought to have his head in a noose at the end of a rope. Mobs were got up by leading men and did not consist of the poorest class. The sons of some of the richest men in Boston used to come in person to attack him when speaking. He had been 'egged' from top to toe till he was the colour 'of that paper' (pointing to a yellow envelope). He had been asked recently to speak at New Orleans. There was a certain degree of generosity in the Southern planters. They valued slavery as an aristocratic institution : if it must go they cared nothing for the compensation. He ended by speaking of the resources of the North and the ease with which they sustained the war.

I had talked last week about Wendell Phillips with William Everett and with Norton and Professor Child.* W. Everett said he knew nothing about him ; he had never heard him or read his speeches. Evidently regards him as beyond the pale. Child called him a firebrand — too bitter and personal. Norton recommended me strongly to see him and said his eloquence derives largely from his personal charm. Some talk of his going to England as a Commissioner to explain the Northern case.

Norton showed me Mr. Everett's declaration of willingness to serve against a 'servile insurrection' : 'Sir, I am no soldier', he said, 'my education has been very unmilitary, but I would shoulder a musket and strap a rifle to my back to suppress a servile insurrection'. This was in 1856 and it has hurt Mr. Everett ever since.

SUNDAY, SEPTEMBER 6

Boston

Found Norton at home : he read me an article of his on relations between England and the United States : very decided as to our iniquities on the pirate question. But the article was mainly to declare that the Americans do not want to go to war with England. He asked whether that was my experience. I said yes. After church went to the Everetts to dine. After dinner I retired to read Wendell Phillips's speeches on my bed till 5.30 when I joined Mr. E.

I may here describe Mr. Everett. He is strongly built and middle sized, grey curly hair, eyes weak from much reading, in speaking shows his lower teeth.

We talked of F. L. Olmsted. Norton told this story to me. Olmsted was with Grant in his tent when a lady came in with some request. Grant, leaning his hand on the table and in an awkward manner, as he always is with ladies, said it could not be managed. She met Olmsted later and told him it was a pity that affairs were not under better hands in the west because Grant's habits were bad, she having herself seen him unable to stand without holding the table.[18]

Mrs. Hale (Mr. Everett's sister) is a very lively old woman and excellent story teller. She is now very big and looks old without a cap and her plain iron grey hair. But she is kindness and cheeriness itself. Edward Everett, Edward Hale (her son) and William Everett joined us. We had a good evening (chopped melon and cookies and currant top buns for tea) and intelligent talk. Hale told us of his voting for Lincoln, when he took his little girl (five years old) to impress upon her a great political event. Mrs. Hale described the old mode of voting when the leaders were present. She told how she remembered seeing the foundations of the buildings on the Capitol. Nathan Hale, another nephew of Edward Everett, came and proposed my going with him and a party to Shoal Islands.

SUNDAY, SEPTEMBER 6

Letter to the aunts

Revere House, Boston

My dear aunts, I had a very interesting day yesterday and was going to insert it in my journal in due form, but I think I may as well write it home to you, only asking you to send on the letter finally to my mother that I may have it to insert in my journal afterwards. I had a letter to Mrs. Stowe who lives at Andover. I walked up to Mrs. Stowe's house and found from her husband, Professor Stowe, that she was away at 'the beach', as they call the seaside here. I talked with Professor Stowe for some time and he told me his views of England and what Lord Palmerston and Lord Russell had said to him when he was there. He found that Lord Palmerston knew much more about American affairs than Lord Russell, which rather surprised him. I thought Professor Stowe rather pompous and anxious to show what great people he knew in England.

In the cars on the way back to Boston from Andover an incident happened which would astonish some people in England, though after being a few weeks here nothing of this sort surprises me. At one of the stations a man got in and sat down opposite me in workman's dress and looking much like a mechanic in Lancashire. I began talking

18. This story is typical of the many in circulation about Grant's drinking habits; it is established that there was little substance to them during the Civil War period. Lincoln always treated such stories with contempt – he would ask what whisky Grant drank so that he could send some barrels of it to his other generals.

to him and he confided to me in the course of our talk that in his family, out of seven brothers and brothers-in-law, six had been to the war, he being the only one who had not been and that because of weak health. He had also had an uncle and some cousins at the war. Of his brothers and brothers-in-law, one had died of cholera after going through thirteen battles, one is on his back for life with a wound, another wounded less seriously, two have got their discharge after serving for the time stipulated, and one is still at the war. How deep are the convictions of these people. This man told me he had not voted for Lincoln; and yet what sacrifices he has now made and how proud he is for the sake of the Union. I hope you have read Mr. Lincoln's letter to the Illinois meeting.

I bought yesterday Wendell Phillips's speeches which you would be very interested to read. He is pungent in his remarks and it is amusing to read his bitter attacks on Mr. Everett who has always been one of the temporizers with slavery although he is now heart and soul for the war. Great efforts are being made for the education of the freedmen. I think an English subscription ought to be set up to aid this, if only to show that we are not all pro-slavery men like The Times *and the* Saturday Review. *As to* The Times — *once it sees that the North is winning it will in my opinion go round like a weather-cock.*

The weather just now is superb. The maple trees are just turning crimson which is one of the most beautiful features in the scenery of this part of America.

MONDAY, SEPTEMBER 7

Boston

Went to see Professor Child. He read me an extract from a Vicksburg letter giving me an account of the excesses of U.S. troops on the abandoned plantations. When not abandoned they are not ill-treated. But Jeff. Davis's* and his brother Joe's were made clean work of.

Called at the book store and bought Whittier's *Ichabod*. After dinner Child took me to a Latin recitation — first of the term for the sophomores or second year men.

TUESDAY, SEPTEMBER 8 to
SATURDAY, SEPTEMBER 12

Got my goods together and went to look up Nathan Hale to start for Shoal Islands. To Portsmouth by train, whence down the river Piscataqua in the *Island Belle* with the mainsails flapping. During the trip came news from the war of Northern successes — the capture of Morris Island off Charleston and

View over the River Piscataqua. Sketch by Yates Thompson, September 10, 1863, Appledore.

Burnside's* Occupation of Knoxville; also the occupation of Chattanooga[19] by General Rosecrans.

SUNDAY, SEPTEMBER 13

New Haven, Connecticut

Called at Summer Street yesterday before leaving Boston for the second time. W. Everett accompanied me to the station and saw me off, introducing me to the manager of the line, a shrewd white-haired man who said that England was behaving badly, but he thought this was from ignorance. I got to New Haven at 8.00 p.m., five and a half hours from Boston. A good many black people got in at Hartford — no difficulty.

Read Sumner's speech: it is very cogent and will have an effect in England: guess it will stop the Ironclads.

I proceeded this morning with a letter from Mr. White to Professor Fisher's* at the north end of New Haven — a fleshy, bald man who, having a cold, had cut church. I sat with him for some time — talked about Sumner's speech, Everett and copperheads at Yale, of whom there are a considerable number, Calhoun* 'the father of all lies' having been there. Everett is considered to be a 'holiday orator': he wants the intrepidity of 'such men as Lord Grey'. 'Sumner is very able,' said Fisher, 'but too fanatical about slavery.'

I sauntered into the square and was going to church when a stout, red-bearded man in a straw hat accosted me, named Professor Silliman — he turned out to be brother-in-law to Professor Fisher. He took me to hear Professor Dwight who discoursed on the character of the apostles. After service we went to his house for dinner. Professor Silliman's sister, Mrs. Trumbull, said Lincoln

19. General Rosecrans, driving General Bragg's army south into Georgia, occupied Chattanooga, Tennessee. Bragg then counter-attacked and defeated the Unionist Army of the Cumberland at the Battle of Chickamauga, south of Chattanooga. The Army of the Cumberland was then besieged in Chattanooga until rescued by Grant at the Battle of Chattanooga, November 23, 24 and 25, 1863.

was gaining ground every day. Professor Silliman is very firm about the iniquity of England in the early granting of belligerency to the Rebels: he believes that Sumner speaks the mind of the Government and that if the Ironclads get out war will be declared. After dinner we went to Professor Silliman's father's* house. The old gentleman, who is eighty-five years old, was in England in 1805 and went from Liverpool to Manchester by stage-coach. He had been in Cornwall to see the mines and on his return journey thence to Portsmouth he saw Nelson just about to go aboard the *Victory*: 'Nelson looked much worn down having just been across the Atlantic and back after the French fleet.'

Professor Silliman's father is a splendid specimen of an old Yankee and a regular patriarch with thirty grandchildren. It is very interesting seeing the interior of so many houses as I do. The Sillimans are a charming family party. People would not talk of the Yankees as they do in England if they knew what they were really like.

MONDAY, SEPTEMBER 14

Went over the Yale buildings with Professor Fisher. At the Treasurer's office we went upstairs into two rooms where are Trumbull's war pictures – a portrait of Governor Trumbull, Governor of Connecticut, the only governor sent out to a colony by England who abided by the Revolution and remained governor of a State – and Trumbull's portrait of Washington. We also saw a portrait of Professor Silliman senior, whom I saw last night, the 'father of chemistry' in this country and conductor of the *Chemical Journal* for forty years.

I made my way to Professor Fisher's at 1.30 p.m., buying a berth (No. 4) on the New York boat by the way at Beecher's grocery store. Found Silliman there and Mrs. Fisher, a pretty but delicate looking woman, and Geordy their boy. Joined at dinner by Professor Thakster (Latin), a shrewd man. We talked of Seward in connection with his letter just published and read by me today. In November 1860 Fisher met Seward soon after he made a speech at New York in which he said there was no danger of war. Fisher said 'Is that your deliberate opinion, Sir?' He said it was and that the Southern explosion, which had been very great on the news of the election of Lincoln, was diminishing fast. Fisher talked of Lincoln and said his main daily recreation is to read a few pages of Yankee stories which he enjoys amazingly. He is very conscious of his defects. A lady who talked with him recently told Fisher that Lincoln said he should not like to travel in Europe. 'Why?', she asked. Because he did not know 'enough of history to enjoy the monuments and antiquities' and because he was 'not a model President of the U.S. – too rough and unpolished'. This is authentic from a lady who had a talk with Lincoln lately (a Mrs. Forbes). Fisher talked with J. C. Breckinridge just before the War broke out. He was recommending still at that time that the forts should not be reinforced and that there was no danger. Yet all the time he was probably 'in the secrets of the cabal'.

After dinner (at which we had sweet potatoes and Delaware grapes) I got back to the hotel and there came Mr. Gilman, librarian, who took me a walk up Hillhouse Avenue and by Tutors Walk, a shady lane up a slope from which is seen the western plain and the Western Rock where the Regicides hid; and through apple trees and above the wooded country we saw a gorgeous evening sun. We crossed the hill and back to the east side of it with a view of the Eastern Rock. New Haven is a considerable manufacturing town. Whitney, the inventor of the cotton gin, was a New Haven man : this invention contributed to the causes of the War because it made slavery so profitable.

BOOK II

SEPTEMBER 15 – NOVEMBER 15

Editor's Introduction

BOOK II of the diaries starts on September 15 in New York and describes a long journey which ended in Louisville, Kentucky, on November 15. The New York visit was disappointing because letters of introduction to General McClellan and to Horace Greeley,* the polemical and strongly political editor of *The New York Tribune*, drew blank. After a few days in Philadelphia our traveller, inspired probably by Olmsted's book, set out to explore the eastern part of Maryland to see for himself how slavery looked in practice. He found it in process of disintegration.

Then he went down to Washington. He was eager to see the Union's armies in action; but first of all he wanted to enlarge his knowledge of the country and see the rapidly expanding West. So on October 7 he started out from Washington, D.C., on a journey by rail and river through the states of West Virginia, Ohio, Michigan, Illinois and Wisconsin to the fringe of Minnesota; and then down the River Mississippi by steamboat to St. Louis. At St. Louis he turned back towards the east, crossed the River Ohio and came to Louisville, Kentucky. There on November 15 he took the first step in a friendship, which stood him later in good stead, by making a call on Dr. J. S. Newberry, head of the United States Sanitary Commission in the West. As will be seen in Book III of the diaries, it was only with the assistance of Dr. Newberry that he was able to achieve his ambition and reach the battlefront — and thus by a remarkable stroke of good fortune obtain a grandstand seat at one of the most spectacular battles of history.

He got to Chattanooga just in the nick of time. Dr. Newberry at the eleventh hour smuggled him into the Sanitary Commission and brought him from Nashville to Chattanooga, where they both arrived on the evening of November 22. After breakfast on the morning of November 23 Yates

[75]

Thompson walked out to Fort Wood, where General Grant had his headquarters, and he took up a position there shortly before the first Unionist attack was launched. But the story of Chattanooga is told in Book III.

Two subjects are treated in this introduction to Book II — the first, slavery emancipation in relation to the situation in eastern Maryland; and the second, the U.S. Sanitary Commission without whose good offices my great uncle would never have reached Chattanooga at all.

It is needless to say that slavery was a subject of intense interest and importance for Yates Thompson. He wanted to find out all he could about it, conditioned as he was by talking with his abolitionist friends in Boston and by reading Olmsted's fascinating book.

Travelling in a steamboat in Chesapeake Bay, he was shocked and surprised by the conversation of a Methodist preacher who insisted that African slavery was divinely inspired. It must be remembered that in the Southern States, the slaves, numbering about four million, almost equalled the free population. The Southerners believed that their economy, and their whole way of life, depended for survival upon the continuance in perpetuity of the system of African slavery. An ever present nightmare was the possibility of a 'servile insurrection'; and there was deep fear of the horrors that supposedly would follow emancipation — a fear that in the event proved groundless because the liberated slaves behaved on the whole with unexpected restraint. It is not surprising, however, that the abolitionists inspired such passionate loathing in the South or that opinion in the North was confused and divided about the problem of slavery.

Lincoln himself, there is no doubt, detested slavery. But this great man was a rare combination of qualities. A compassionate man who hated cruelty and injustice, he was also tolerant, generous and above all practical. He believed that emancipation, immediate and total, as pressed upon him by the abolitionists, was not only impossible to bring about, but unjust to many and dangerous for everyone. What he tried to establish was an agreed programme of emancipation, over a period, with generous compensation to the slave owners. 'Gradual and not sudden emancipation', he said, 'is better for all.'

When Lincoln led the Republicans to victory in 1860 emancipation was not in the programme of the party. The issue was whether or not the area of slavery should be allowed to spread into the newly formed States of the Union. In his first inaugural address Lincoln said that 'he had no purpose directly or indirectly to interfere with the institution of slavery in the States where it exists'. This was confirmed in a special session of Congress in July 1861.

On the bare facts alone it is quite difficult to explain why the Southern States decided to secede and face the fearful risk of war, just because Lincoln won the presidential election in 1860 against a split vote in the Democratic

Party. There was no immediate threat to the Southern planters' cherished way of life. But over a long period passions and fears in the Southern States had become inflamed almost to breaking point and there came a time when neither caution nor sane counsels could prevail. The final decisions were emotional rather than rational. But how many decisions for war are based upon reason?

Nevertheless, by opting for war the Southern States sealed the fate of the institution they were trying to save. 'Secession and rebellion, designed and begun by the Southern leaders to extend and perpetuate slavery, proved the most powerful agency for its swift destruction.'[1] Slavery became a casualty of war. Wherever the Union armies moved into or occupied Confederate territory slavery fell apart. When their owners had fled those slaves who had been left behind sought refuge with the invaders. Slaves being enemy property were confiscated if used for purposes of war. They were called 'contrabands' and put into camps or employed by the Unionists on necessary labour. The Fugitive Slave Act became a dead letter. Where the Union armies went they were followed by long lines of fugitive or abandoned slaves, often suffering dreadful hardships and an embarrassment to the armies in the field. Slavery fell to pieces under the pragmatic processes of 'military emancipation' and the pieces could never be put together again.

As the War laboured on, opinion in favour of freeing the slaves made rapid progress in the North and also in the loyal border States where slavery still prevailed. A milestone was reached when Lincoln, using the wide powers he possessed as Commander-in-Chief of the nation's armed forces in wartime, issued his famous Proclamation of September 1862. This came into force on January 1, 1863, and it sounded the doom of African slavery in America, since it committed the Union to a cause from which it could never retreat unless defeated in the field. But the Proclamation only applied to the States in rebellion on January 1, 1863. Throughout 1862 Lincoln did his utmost to persuade the loyal slave States to accept a formula for gradual emancipation with compensation to the owners of slaves. The negotiations with Maryland and the State of Delaware dragged on into 1863; but in April 1862 Lincoln was able to sign an Act of Congress freeing all slaves in the District of Columbia with compensation paid at $300 a slave. Loyal West Virginia was then admitted as a new State into the Union in June 1863 after accepting a scheme for gradual emancipation. Not long afterwards Maryland and Missouri altered their own State constitutions to bring slavery to an end within their borders.

What Yates Thompson saw in eastern Maryland in September 1863 was the disintegration of slavery resulting from military measures for the enlistment

1. *Cambridge Modern History*, 1905 edn., Volume VII, Chapter XVIII.

and training of negro troops – it was a form of 'military emancipation'. Lincoln's Proclamation contained a provision as follows : 'And further I declare and make known that such persons (slaves) of suitable condition shall be received into the armed service of the United States.' The enlistment of negro soldiers evoked the most violent reactions in the South Jefferson. Davis said : 'Our own detestation of those who have attempted the most execrable measure recorded in the history of guilty man is tempered by profound contempt for the impotent rage which it discloses.' The Confederate War Department issued an order that Union officers commanding negro soldiers should be executed if captured. Although the Confederate armies made wholesale use of slaves in various military labours, even General Robert E. Lee went so far as to accuse the North of trying to start a 'servile war, which is worse than that of the savage, in as much as it superadds other horrors to the indiscriminate slaughter of ages, sexes and conditions.'[2]

At the time when Yates Thompson was in Maryland the Federal Government was pressing forward with the enlistment and training of black troops as a matter of urgency. It was for the prosecution of the War that the special powers of the President were invoked to enable the enlistment of negro slaves in eastern Maryland, a part of the State that was never touched directly by the War. The eastern Maryland slave-owners who received their compensation, arbitrarily assessed though it may have been, were luckier than others – for in the end emancipation without compensation was decreed by the State Government of Maryland.

At first race prejudice in the Federal armies raised objection in various places to negroes in uniform. But by the middle of 1863 the North was raising a number of negro regiments, and the white soldiers who had at first been bitter about the idea adjusted themselves in due course. In the end more than 150,000 negroes were employed in the Federal Armies. Most of the negro regiments were confined to garrison duty and other non-combatant activities. But some units went into the firing line and acquitted themselves well.

Before finally taking leave of the subject of slavery I must quote a few sentences from a lecture given by my great-uncle at Cambridge early in 1865. By then he had reached the age of twenty-six, and he was making an appeal for donations to the Freedman's Aid Society – 'a society', as he observed, 'to help the emancipated slaves in the Southern States who are destitute through no fault of their own.' He continued :

'A civil war has arisen in a kindred community. At its outbreak that community contained four millions of negro or mulatto slaves. Wherever the Unionists have conquered they have liberated the slave population. In

2. ibid.

November last Mr. Jefferson Davis estimated that two millions out of the original four millions had been emancipated or, as the expression is, "stolen" by the Unionists. In the city of Savannah all last year negro slavery continued as usual. Artisans and field hands, and their wives and children, were bought and sold in the market. But in December General Sherman and his army entered Savannah and no one will ever again be bought or sold in that city.

But what of the former slaves? They are poor and ignorant and they have been degraded by long bondage. They do not know which way to turn. How are their needs met by their emancipators? Mr. Lincoln's government allots them land and opens to them all lawful occupations; and the people form societies in their aid. Many men and women have left the peace and comfort of their Northern homes and gone to assist and educate these destitute people with all the spirit and devotion of Howard the philanthropist or Florence Nightingale. It is in aid of this work that a branch society has been established in England. We have already sent £20,000; and perhaps that seems to you a large sum. But it is to be remembered that about two years ago there was great distress in the county of Lancaster where I reside. There was a considerable English subscription in aid of the cotton operatives and it was supplemented by a gift of £55,000 from America. I think I am within the mark when I say that £20,000 from prosperous England is a small and paltry gift.'

The second subject to be treated here is the United States Sanitary Commission. This organization derived its name from a voluntary body which was first established to introduce conditions of hygiene into army camps which were pest houses of dysentery and typhoid. Early in 1861 that remarkable man, Frederick Law Olmsted, was given leave from his duties at Central Park by the City of New York to become General Secretary of the Sanitary Commission, which he developed in the space of two years into an immensely powerful agency for the relief of suffering among the troops. I quote from one of the lectures given by Yates Thompson in England in 1864:

'There is a society in the free States called the Sanitary Commission — its object to succour the sick and wounded soldiers of both sides — its funds derived from voluntary subscriptions of money and in kind. To show its extent I will mention one fact. There was a Fancy Fair held in New York last year — one of several throughout the country — in aid of the Sanitary Commission. This single Fair produced over one million dollars net. Pretty well, ladies, for one Fancy Fair.'

[79]

Another part of the Sanitary Commission's activities was the distribution of supplies to the soldiers, supplementing what was available to them from army sources. Storehouses were opened at strategic points; agents with waggonloads of supplies travelled with the armies; and everything sent to the soldiers, from drinks to soap, went under the name of 'sanitary stores'. The Commission also opened soldiers' homes and rest houses; cared for the convalescents discharged from military hospitals and added to the stores of the hospitals themselves; delivered bandages and medical supplies; and in short made good the deficiencies of the Medical Bureau and other government agencies in almost every field. After the Battle of Antietam in September 1862 the Commission began to develop its relief activities at the battlefronts. The Army Medical Department never became adequate for what was needed; and to the end of the War the Sanitary Commission continued its good works on the battlefield as well as in the hospitals and camps.

Another organization, known as the Christian Commission, grew up beside the Sanitary Commission. It too was bountifully financed from voluntary sources. It grew out of the Y.M.C.A. and its aims were primarily religious and moral. The Sanitary Commission looked after the soldiers' bodily needs; the Christian Commission was to provide for their spiritual wellbeing. There came to be a certain amount of overlapping of the work of the two commissions; and in the later period of the War, when it had raised huge sums from the various religious denominations, the Christian Commission competed with the Sanitary Commission in the distribution of food, clothing and hospital stores. These two great voluntary bodies performed a vital part in the War and in due time the Sanitary Commission gave birth to the American Red Cross.

The Diary

SEPTEMBER 15 – NOVEMBER 15

TUESDAY, SEPTEMBER 15

New York

This is a good day on which to begin a new book of my Diary. At New Haven yesterday at 10.00 p.m. I drove in an open carriage past Professor Fisher's house along Chapel Street which runs the length of New Haven to the pier : thence by Continental Steamboat asleep to New York.

I stupidly relied upon the Express for my luggage and it did not arrive until 1 p.m. here at the Brevoort House.

I went into a theatre on the west side of Broadway where I saw wonderful rope dancing by a girl : audience near me all Germans. After this went to St. Nicholas Hotel, where I was met by Professor White who discoursed on politics. He insisted much on England's danger from U.S. privateers in case of war. Walked with him as far as Fourth Avenue.

Yates Thompson's boat ticket from New Haven to New York.

Am slightly depressed by two vain calls on General McClellan at 22 31st Street West and Colonel Aspinwall at 101 Street adjoining 33 University Place. Horace Greeley is also away from New York.

Found a card from C. A. Saunders at Brevoort House. Was he the fellow I whopped at Harrow for drinking whisky in a barn?

TUESDAY, SEPTEMBER 15

Letter to brother Sam

The Brevoort House, New York

I hope to goodness that mercenary war breeder of Liverpool, Mr. Laird, is not to be allowed to send out the Rams. I believe the Yankees would be made very savage and probably declare war on us. What business have we making a navy for people who have no open port and no available prize courts? It is scandalous work and if we went to war on such a question I would sooner go into the American army than into ours. If the law is not strong enough to prevent such atrocities, why is it not made so? I blush for my country when I think of the moral support we are giving to these brutal slave owners, about whom people who know anything, American or English, have only one opinion. The Times, I see has gone round about the Rams and wants them stopped, which looks as if people are coming to their senses, and I hope it may be so. You see my side goes on winning – Chattanooga,[1] Knoxville[2] and Morris Island[3] are of the utmost importance and comparatively bloodless victories.

WEDNESDAY, SEPTEMBER 16

Down town by Bowery cars (negro woman in car) to Richard Irvin, Esq.'s office. Found him in, an oldish man of the British merchant class with fingers of right hand shrunk and stiff in a bent position. He asked me out to Oyster Bay.

I was leaving his office when his son, Al, overtook me and suggested lunch. We went down a crowded street where people were buying and selling gold, and into Delmonico's where we had a good dinner. Al left me in the Exchange news room to read *The Times*, etc.

I passed in Broadway what I supposed to be the funeral of a negro officer. Procession of negroes, two with swords drawn and in uniform. Twenty coaches with mostly coloured mourners but some whites. This I took to be an event in New York. Al Irvin later confirmed this. Crossed the ferry in a large covered steamboat and waited half an hour for the Syosset train. The Irvin house is only built for summer with lots of window and a piazza in front and a billiard room behind. Tea and billiards.

THURSDAY, SEPTEMBER 17

Oyster Bay

Breakfast at 6.30 a.m. and Mr. Irvin and Al went off to New York. I sailed the *Wideawake* (a 22 foot boat with mainsail and jib) down the bay with the

1. Chattanooga was occupied by Rosecrans in September 1862 (see note 19, page 69).
2. Knoxville, east Tennessee, was occupied by General Burnside with a small force as a first step to free east Tennessee from the Confederate forces.
3. Morris Island – an island off Charleston, South Carolina, taken by the Unionists.

wind and beat up. Some fine houses on the banks. The island is fertile. Raced a manure schooner up.

FRIDAY, SEPTEMBER 18

Oyster Bay

Breakfast again at 6.30 a.m. and caught the train to New York with Mr. Irvin. He had emigrated as a young man from Scotland. He never votes here. He is for abolition, but considers the Government tyrannical. He is angry with Mr. Chase* – who is 'moulding his finance measures with a view to the Presidential election'. 'The Government ought not to have the control of the currency. Government borrowed one million dollars last week from the Bank with which

Yates Thompson's sketch of Oyster Bay, Long Island.

I am connected,' he said : 'these loans are very profitable to the banks. Government pay interest in gold and begin payments from the time the bargain is concluded though they only draw the money by instalments. The Long Island farmers are thrifty and prosperous, owe no money on their farms, mostly Democrats before the War, now solid for the Union.' He said : 'No wonder the English go with the South. England and Paris are full of runaway planters whose only politics consist in staying in Europe with a whole skin and touting for their friends in the South'. 'This', as I observed to him, 'is mean work.'

SATURDAY, SEPTEMBER 19

Philadelphia, Pennsylvania

Rose to a cold morning with thermometer twenty-five degrees below what it was yesterday. By expensive carriage to the Cortland St. ferry. Great crowd in the streets near the ferry. Grey-haired New York Democrat sat next me reading *The World* : puzzled about the emancipation proclamation : surprised by my account of the negro funeral in New York : thinks negroes are meant to be slaves. Man sitting in front of us reading *The Tribune* – he had five brothers in the war, two 'found a soldier's grave', one a cripple, one 'skedaddled, having had enough of it'. The New York Democrat said there was a remarkable revival of commerce just now, New York being full of solid western men come with orders – also many from New Orleans, Tennessee, Kentucky, etc.

Went to Henry Cramond's office and thence to his house. Was introduced to old lady (86) his mother. She despairs of the country and loves England and said to Cramond : 'He tells me England is flourishing, I'm glad to hear it, glad to hear it.' Henry Cramond is a man of fifty-four – has been something of a fop. Is a friend of the English Consul : has dined with Lord Lyons and with General McClellan. Knows General Meade*: showed me his father's house opposite to General Meade's father's house. We talked some time chiefly of the War. Walked with me to his club where had a cup of tea and thence to the theatre where a Mrs. Perrins acted Lucrezia Borgia and a Senorita Cubas danced. At the most melodramatic part of L.B. a girl near us cried out 'I am going to die' and hurried out of the theatre. Cramond gave me instances of Baltimore men imprisoned for refusing to swear allegiance. One was kept in a fort for a year. Soldiers outside theatre looking for men without passes.

[85]

SATURDAY, SEPTEMBER 19

Letter to mother

Continental Hotel, Philadelphia

Philadelphia is only one hundred miles from Gettysburg, where the fighting was so desperate just over two months ago. But the thronged streets and theatres here don't look at all like exhaustion and I am quite staggered by your letter and by your doubts about 'the pleasure of freedom in the North for a slave, as compared with slavery in the South'. If you really think slavery pleasanter, all I say is you don't know what slavery is; and if you won't read and know what slavery is and won't believe me who has read and got a certain idea about it (and also seen 'this terrible ill-treatment in the north' the result of which is that the black population looks tidy and thriving) — then you are, I say, intractable, and all I can do is to assure you of my own conviction and trust to events to bring you round.

I am so certain myself of the good to humanity of this War that, if the North were not winning, I should be inclined to volunteer myself and have a shot at some of those accursed people whom you are all praising so loudly. Indeed, I have a good mind to do it now, just to show that all Englishmen are not so selfish and ignorant as most of them seem to be. I don't believe one could be killed in a better cause. However, I am going to the West first and I start on Tuesday.

I found nobody at home in New York except Mr. Irvin, who took me out to his country place on Long Island for a couple of days. Then I came on here. Mr. Cramond, a friend of Uncle Robert, is very civil to me here. He knows General Meade and recommends me to visit that army. I am going West first however. I want to have a good idea of all the country before I see the armies in the field.

SUNDAY, SEPTEMBER 20

Wrote letters and then called on J. W. Field to whom I am recommended by C. E. Norton. He has a peaked and long beard, grey towards the end. Been in Europe till the War broke out — a thick-and-thin Unionist, confident of final, though not speedy, success. Met Cramond and into a handsome early English church: sermon on selfishness by a pompous man. Then to the Club (about 250 members) and sat with Cramond in the private room with Stuart's portrait of Washington on the wall. In came Mr. Cortwright, English Consul, a stout, curly-haired, florid man with the look of a man of pleasure. Also, came E. E. Law, an old man originally Scotch. We had an exquisite dinner — reed birds, a great delicacy, then madeira from one of the two demijohns of wine secured by

[86]

Cramond. Conversation soon settled down from watering places in Europe to politics. The Pennsylvania Legislature is now disreputable. The best men do not think it worthwhile taking part in it. Cortwright and Law settled down to an argument or rather an exposition from Law with occasional statements from Cortwright. Cortwright is beneath contempt, knows no facts and seems incapable of grasping them. Has been Consul in Granada and talked snobbishly about the Prince of Wales. Knew nothing of history, remarking: 'I consider you have to go through a certain number of phases so that you will arrive at a constitutional monarchy.' Cramond and Law think that no compromise should be made with slavery now.

TUESDAY, SEPTEMBER 22

Monday and Tuesday have been two important days for me. Cramond called for me early yesterday and we walked by Independence Hall to get

> ## PASS.
> ## U. S. ARMY GENERAL HOSPITAL,
> ### CHESTNUT HILL.
>
> Admit *Mr Thompson and Mr C Newhall*
>
> By Order of
> ### Surgeon Commanding Hospital.
> *Chas B Greenleaf*
> *Austin Infantry*
> *Executive Offr*

Yates Thompson's pass to the US General Hospital, Philadelphia.

tickets for the Girard College and Penitentiary. Thence to the Athenaeum where Cramond put my name down. The Penitentiary, one of the first established on the solitary system — seven radiating wards from a central hall, whence the eye commands the whole. Prisoners soon ask for work and many learn to read. Cramond enlarged on the growth of the city.

Called on Dr. Furness.* He showed me a photograph of a negro's back, a horrid sight. We talked an hour or so, Dr. Furness expressing disgust at England. We walked on to J. W. Field's. Mrs. Field is a delicate-looking woman. Her father was a Virginian planter but their plantation is by this time destroyed. Field is a strong abolitionist, has travelled much, at present assisting the Newhalls in their Pennsylvania Sugar Refinery. He gave us capri and asti wine, Gruyère and English cheese. After dinner found Miss Peters just from Europe, a very stylish young woman, and Mrs. Lister (Dr. Furness's daughter). Mrs. Lister said that Miss Peters was a traitress.

Today at Field's office by 9.00 a.m. Went over the refinery. Said Newhall to Field: 'We're about making our fortunes.'

Charley Newhall took me in a 'spider trap' with one trotting pony to the negro camp of the 6th Regiment. Over the crest of the road we saw, beyond a slight ravine, tents for 800 men on the bare slope. Walked about the tents. Great joking and laughing: 'Oh you rabel, you rabel', said one man to another from under one of the tents. They keep their arms wonderfully clean. Guard turned out very promptly and everything spick and span. Thence I went to Chestnut Hill U.S. Army Hospital. Everything beautiful to see — no limit to quantity of food for the men.

THURSDAY, SEPTEMBER 24
Barnham's Hotel, Baltimore, Maryland

Wrote to Henry Bright about Philadelphia.

Talked with a young officer, a Marylander who had had Southern sympathies until Fort Sumpter. He has been in all the Potomac army's battles, was under Sedgewick at Fredericksburg[4] – describes the retreat thence after Burnside's* defeat as most perilous. The whole of Sedgewick's division defiled through a small gap in the enemy pickets and marched five miles to the river. He recognized a cousin among the Rebel wounded at Gettysburg. He believes in negro troops.

Went out by Sutaw Street to the negro camp and listened to talk between a Mr. McKinn and a Colonel Burney. McKinn just back from Washington where he talked with Stanton.* Stanton is for radical measures about slavery. A depot has been set up for recruiting at Harper's Ferry and a camp at Fortress Monroe for East Maryland. Overwhelmed with recruits. McKinn said that

4. The Battle of Fredericksburg. In November 1862 the Federal Army of the Potomac, 120,000 strong, attacked Lee holding an immensely strong position at Fredericksburg. The battle was a disastrous failure for the Unionists and the Army of the Potomac suffered more than 12,000 casualties.

Stanton had declared to him that Burney was to be made Brigadier-General with chief command of recruiting in Maryland. McKinn says it is a race between Maryland and Tennessee, which shall emancipate first. Stanton's scheme is 300 dollars compensation to the master on the enlistment of a slave.

FRIDAY, SEPTEMBER 25

Steamboat Kent, Chesapeake Bay

Left Baltimore at 7.00 a.m. Talked with Mr. Ball, a Methodist preacher — a little man with iron grey hair, bushy eybrows, white tie and dirty black appearance. Lives at Baltimore.

Said he: 'I believe slavery of the black man to be a divine institution. As all Englishmen do you, Sir, as I hope, believe in your English bible. Go to Genesis tenth. You find there how Ham and his children were made servants of Japhet, from whom you, Sir, are descended, and also of Shem. When Providence's time for the setting free of the negroes comes it will be revealed some way to the slave-owners.'

I said: 'That may apply, Sir, to negroes but how about half-breeds?'

'I should like to have time to explain that to you and also more about the Divine Right of slavery. The slave, Sir, draws his slavery from his mother. The

General Ambrose E. Burnside, defeated commander of the Federal troops at the Battle of Fredericksburg. 'Sideburns' were named after him. (Courtesy of the National Archive.)

[89]

father may alter his colour, but if the mother is a slave that is enough.' I asked him about the beating of women. 'Sir, you must go to first principles. I believe that punishment is required in all states of society. You send a woman to the Penitentiary. We take a whip to her and have done with it.' I cannot describe the fiendish eagerness with which he insisted on these dogmas.

FRIDAY, SEPTEMBER 25

Easton, Maryland

Got to the pier at 3.40 p.m. and drove up three miles to Easton. Went to Henry Goldsborough's house. He told me about his position as leader of the abolition movement in Maryland. He considers slavery wrong economically. He owns twelve negroes but prefers letting them out. He would like to get rid of his negroes entirely, but they decline to go. He himself has always been 'loyal'. Once, early in the War, the flag of secession was displayed in the town. He was at that time in the Legislature and he was threatened with hanging, by letter and otherwise. At one time he was President of the Senate. Met Dr. Chamberlayne, a medical man, in the street. Chamberlayne said : 'Three years ago, that boy,' pointing to a negro boy of sixteen, 'would have fetched sixteen hundred dollars. Now he might be worth one hundred dollars, but I would be sorry to give half a dollar for him. At a sale a few weeks ago in Easton a woman and two children fetched one hundred dollars.'

SATURDAY, SEPTEMBER 26

Out after breakfast, visited the market. Lots of negroes, mainly free. Federal soldier passed with loaded revolver after deserters. Goldsborough came up and told me that 700 slaves in Easton had enlisted in the last fortnight. I rode down to the pier to ticket my trunk which is to go to Annapolis. Overtook two soldiers, one in the infantry with a fixed bayonet, and one in the cavalry, with six deserters taken in the neighbourhood.

SATURDAY, SEPTEMBER 26

Letter to brother Sam

Island Creek, Maryland

I have got into the strangest place yet. Look at the map and you will find Baltimore on Chesapeake Bay. I left there yesterday at 7.00 a.m. by steamboat. We called at Annapolis, the state capital of Maryland, and got to Easton, which you will find on the eastern shore of the Bay, at 3.00 p.m. I was attracted to this place by having been told by my friend Hammond of Trinity College that he had relatives, whose names he gave me, living in the neighbourhood. I was curious to see a rural district of a slave state and the working of the 'peculiar institution'. Easton is a country town of two thousand inhabitants. It is in Talbot County, of which the population is about eight thousand whites and six thousand coloured, of whom three thousand are slaves. I found two members of the Hammond family in Easton, one of them being Henry Goldsborough, late President of the Senate of Maryland, an unconditional Union man, and the other the doctor of the village. Henry Goldsborough took me over his farm and told me a good deal about the state of the country. From the steamboat I had seen another steamboat pass us towards Baltimore loaded with negroes for the camp there. These came mainly from Talbot County. The Government is revolutionizing this district by recruiting all negroes who will go, slave or free. The secessionists of the district are rabid about it and even many Union men are aghast. Their corn stands uncut in the fields. I had tea with Henry Goldsborough at Easton last night and met Dr. Chamberlayne who proposed to take me over to his cousin's, twelve miles off, next morning. This morning after breakfast at Easton I looked about the market just opposite the hotel. About half the people were black, the women with coloured handkerchiefs round their heads, turban-wise, the men seedily dressed and all bargaining for sweet potatotes, etc.

The doctor brought his carryall at about 10.00 o'clock and we set off for this place. My companion went half a mile out of his road to show me an old church where is the tombstone of John Thompson of Whitehaven 1742 and of Robert Norris of Liverpool who was going on board his ship at Oxford near here, when the men fired a gun in his honour and the wad hit and killed him. We went on. When carts passed us the negro driver invariably raised his hat and grinned. We were met by an oldish man on a grey pony much excited. He stopped us and said with many lamentations that he had lost three slaves and did not know where it was to stop. Would Government pay him for them? How was he to get a certificate? If they would give him three hundred dollars it was better than nothing. But he had given eight hundred for a boy when quite young. Soon after this we turned out of the road through a gate into an avenue half a mile long of locust trees running between the cornfields up to a wooden house placed prettily among trees and surrounded by turf and looking on the opposite side onto a creek from the Chesapeake Bay which goes along the side of the house. Halfway up the drive we saw the master of the house, James Lloyd Chamberlayne, cutting the corn with two or three slaves and one white man. The master received us with hospitality. We dined at 1.00 p.m. on homely fare — fowls and ham, and sweet potatoes, and oysters from the creek and peaches from the garden. After dinner I tried my hand at corn cutting. Mr. C. has four slaves on the place and one white man as *overseer. When coming into tea we met another cousin, one Sam Chamberlayne, who took us to his house. As we approached the house we saw two urchins, eight or ten years old, with guns. They had been shooting a small white pigeon which they call a dove. We found a Mr. John Kerr, a neighbour and member for Talbot County in the State Legislature. He told us about six deserters who had hidden themselves in his section. They lived there for three weeks without being found. I write this in Mr. Sam Chamberlayne's parlour — he sitting on the other side of the round table, his legs up on a chair towards the wood fire, smoking a cigar and reading the* Baltimore American. *He has lost no slaves yet which is exceptional, but he says he may lose them all any day. They tell him that they will not go but this is rather a sign that they intend to go. Three years ago a boy of sixteen was worth fifteen hundred dollars. A fortnight ago in Easton some slaves were sold, the best getting three hundred dollars. Now they are utterly unsaleable.*

MONDAY, SEPTEMBER 28

Annapolis

I must detail my East Shore experiences while they are fresh. Last night slept in a room with John Kerr at James Lloyd Chamberlayne's house. Woke

Sketch by Yates Thompson of a Maryland slave cabin.

at six o'clock and had a dip in the creek. A white mist rose from the creek. The dew was frosty on the grass. I had my swim, wading out some way in the mud, came in and dressed. James Lloyd met me outside and told me to warm myself. There was a negro paddling up in a canoe. He had been to the meeting at Oxford. 'He has not gone off anyway', was James Lloyd's remark.

Got back to the house for the fag end of prayers and we had breakfast. After breakfast went out with John Kerr and turned down to 'the quarter'. Hesitated a little but finally went up the two wooden steps shown in my sketch into a room ten feet square. Open fireplace with remains of a big log in it ; floor of earth, two windows, one on each side of the building — glass in neither and one with an old shirt hanging across it. To the right partition of wood with cracks in it : through the cracks saw a sort of sleeping place with crinolines lying about. Deal table with ten legs – a few mugs on it and a horn pipe with Union colours on the bowl. Two slaves came in, a one-eyed slave and another. Asked the one-eyed slave if he had spent the night at Oxford at the meeting he said 'yes'. Was there any talk of enlisting? He said 'no', but seemed to be telling a lie. They discussed between themselves a meeting to be held at Oxford tonight, where the children would make speeches which they had learned by heart. How did they feed, I asked? 'Oh very well – corned bread and milk, coffee in harvest time, fifteen pounds of pork a month, some molasses.' They are allowed to travel about, which they are very fond of doing, and going to the meetings at night at Oxford. This would not be allowed in other slave States. Kerr spoke about my talking to the slaves and making a sketch of 'the quarter'. 'If you had done that two years ago, your life would not have been safe. Even now it is not wise. If you went to the meeting in Oxford it would be very dangerous. A man who did that in old times would be taken, handcuffed, to Easton. The mob would collect and his life would be in danger.' I quite believed all this : so much so that I gave up my idea of going to the meeting.

Discussed with John Kerr and J. L. Chamberlayne negro punishments. A boy had run away from Chamberlayne's father. I asked : 'Was he paddled when he came back?' 'No, but he would have been in old times.' What is this paddle like? A flat board like a brush handle with holes in it : after a blow there is a blister to each hole : it is applied on the seat. Some people use a riding whip of cowhide and this is applied on the back. The limit is thirty-nine blows of the paddle : five or six lashes with the whip. They do not paddle women ; but cow-hide them stripped to the waist. A woman was whipped recently at Trappe : she had fought with another. Six months ago a man shot a negro but he was not molested. The negro, badly wounded, ran off to Dr. Chamberlayne's at Easton. This happened on the farm next to James Lloyd's and John Kerr corroborated it.

On the boat talked with Hewlett, a tall young man. He has lost fifty negroes, has thirty-six left. In his opinion the only way with negroes is to be strict. 'I sit in my library with a spy-glass in view of the field. I can see who is loitering. When I catch one I give him hell. I tell you, Sir, they don't like my spy-glass.' He ties his niggers to a tree and whips them with a cowhide whip. He does not like them sneaking off. He told them so: if they *must* enlist, let them tell him and they shall go. Hewlett is going to Baltimore to get white labour. What he wants is the poorest sort of Irish who will work with slaves. He never buys a negro who can read: 'It spoils them.' He is not married but finds plenty of substitutes. He lives in bachelor-style, entertaining the ladies about.

Also talked to a tall bearded man chewing tobacco. He used to live in the south-western part of Missouri. His land was overrun by guerillas: so he migrated to Ohio. He has been at his father's on East Shore since May. His father has no overseer and is too old to attend to his negroes: his crops are halved this year. No one whipped on the farm — 'but we threaten them and curse them all round'. Bad negroes are sold to the South — 'we get extraordinary prices for yellow girls to go South'.

TUESDAY, SEPTEMBER 29

Washington, D.C.

At Wormley's well-known boarding house in Washington kept by a coloured man of that name. Sent following letter to *Daily News*:

I spent the last few days in a farm house in eastern Maryland. The country is flat and cut into strips, or necks as they are called, by creeks from Chesapeake Bay which run into the land and wander through it so that in Talbot County scarcely a farm is without its waterfront and no spot is more than three miles from water. Here the traveller, tired of rail cars and steamboats, has rest.

In eastern Maryland a social change is going on at the moment such as is rare in the life of a nation — the destruction of slavery. Your readers may like to have some account of this. To put the matter shortly the slaves are running away. Young slaves, who three years ago were worth twelve hundred dollars in the villages which I visited, only fetched three hundred dollars three weeks ago and many are hard at work drilling in the coloured camp at Baltimore. There is indignation among the planters, blasphemy in the bar-rooms and serious anxiety as to how the crops can be saved. There is astonishment too at the behaviour of the slaves. They have shown no signs of insubordination. Down to the last moment they cut their maize and eat their corn-cake with their old docility — then they suddenly disappear and their former owner has to be content with a certificate from the Colonel in Baltimore and must just hope for what-ever compensation Government will give. This has all come about within the last three weeks. In a village which I visited a boy of sixteen was sold three weeks ago for three hundred dollars and today slave property in Maryland is unsaleable.

The centre of the matter is the coloured camp in Baltimore. The means employed by Government are steamboats calling at different points along the coast to receive the runaways and carry them off to Baltimore under the United States flag. They may be seen daily in the grey wideawakes and ragged trousers of their slave life marking time and learning their drill before Yankee officers. Their injured workers flock to the camp to get certificates entitling them to receive perhaps three hundred dollars or whatever compensation the Congress will allow them. 'Rebel in de camp! Run him out!' shout the negroes. As I entered one of them said: 'Come to look for slaves? Eh! Reckon you'll not get them here.' The candidates for certificates look very glum as they pass between the grinning ranks of their quondam chattels. All this time on the eastern shore the broad flat fields of maize are ready to be cut and nobody can say how the crop is to be saved in time to get the seed in or indeed whether any of it can be saved at all. The richest planters suffer most. I met one of the larger planters who had lost eighty-five, almost all his able-bodied hands, worth a hundred thousand dollars at the old prices. Another told me he had lost sixteen out of fifty-two and fears that the rest may go any night. Not one of the slave-owners whom I have met believes that the negroes can fight. 'I know the negro, Sir, as well as if I had made him and he'll no more fight than your hat will', said one.

I heard a good deal said about the similarity existing between the lower orders in England and slaves. Considerable delusion seems to exist on this point. An Englishman seems to be presumed by most slave-owners to favour slavery from a similarity of institutions. As to the future supply of labour, there is great anxiety. There will be a great demand for labour in eastern Maryland. It seems reasonable to suppose that the abolition of slavery in the State, which may now be considered beyond doubt, will result in small farms worked by free labour replacing the large slave plantations, improved cultivation and increased population. When once the trying period of transition is passed the State will become far more prosperous than it has been before. If I were to settle in America today either as a labourer or a farmer, I should choose a border slave State as my location.

WEDNESDAY, SEPTEMBER 30

Letter to brother Rodie

Wormley's, Washington

I am in good quarters in a house kept by a coloured man named Wormley. I called this morning on Mr. Wise, son-in-law of Mr. Everett. He was in his office at the Navy Department with a pile of letters before him. He is Chief of Ordnance here. His room contains some specimens of projectiles of fantastic shapes and maps of Charleston and the Mississippi River. The letters seem to be all about guns — hundred pounders and four hundred pounders and gun carriages and schemes for turret ships, etc., etc. I am to dine with him this evening. Washington is a disgusting place.[5] The broad avenues are like deserts, two inches deep in dust all over. Cavalry men are galloping about on the seediest horses in the wildest manner kicking up the dust.

3.00 p.m. Just returned from an excursion with Mr. Wormley to visit a son of Dr. Furness of Philadelphia, who is captain in the 6th Pennsylvania Cavalry. We drove past the Capitol near to which is a rebel prison where we saw the rebel captives sunning themselves behind the bars — a wild looking lot. Saw a civilian prison also.

Crossed the Eastern Branch, a broad river meeting the Potomac a mile or so below the long wooden bridge. Three miles further down river on a height overlooking the Potomac and a wide tract of Virginia, I found the 6th Penn. regiment and Captain Furness having lunch — oysters and peach preserve washed down with Rhine wine and applejack — not bad after a drive in Washington dust. This regiment was in Stoneman's[6] raid, which was a brilliant affair. Furness asked me out to the camp for a few days to see camp life. I think I shall go on Thursday. If it is not windy it will be good fun; if windy the dust will be too much for anything, and if raining so will the mud. The Regiment is there to recoup after long service at the front. Their horses are very sick. Coming down from camp we saw two companies of cavalry marching along the road. The dust lay like snow on their clothes, arms, and horses, whitening their bronzed faces and beards.

This journey delights me more and more. I wish you were all with me; and yet for seeing the country there is nothing like being alone. For the pleasure of my east Maryland trip lay in the insight I got into the farmer life there, which two persons would have failed to get. From the first week I spent at Mr. Everett's I have had a series of scenes each one complete in itself. You remember my week with Mr. White of Keene, N.H., my trip to the Isle of Shoals with Nathan Hale, my day with G. Walker of Springfield and my Oyster Bay visit to Mr. Irvin. Altogether I have spent about a month sleeping under friendly roofs.

5. Washington, at the time of the Civil War, was an unfinished city and its wide streets after rain or snow became rivers of mud. Anthony Trollope, arriving in Washington in December 1862, saw everything through a cloud of dust — but then came some snow 'and Washington assumed its normal winter condition. In walking about one waded as deep in mud as one does in floundering through an ordinary ploughed field.' (From *North America*, 1862.)
6. 'Stoneman's Raid' was a bold exercise. General Stoneman rode right round Lee's army and got within two miles of Richmond.

Secretary of State.

Mr. H. Y. Thompson,
at Wormley's -
I Street -

Mr. Seward sends his card to Yates
Thompson in Washington.

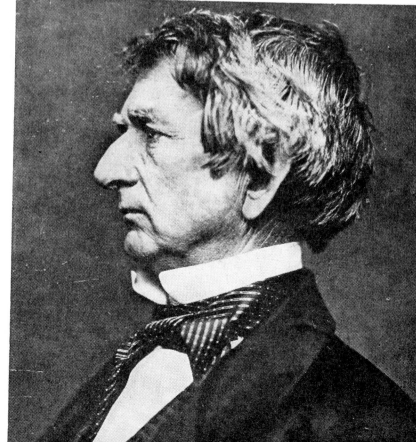

William Henry Seward,
Secretary of State.

Thursday, October 1

3.00 p.m. have just come in from a visit to the 'Contraband Camp'. The latter is a strange sight – about seven hundred and fifty women and children and old men who have been slaves in Virginia sent here by the armies to be supported. They live in shanties and are fed by the Government. The rebels carry all the able-bodied slaves off to the South and leave the sick and infirm. They have a good deal of disease among them. I saw a waggon load of them arrive quite exhausted by the long trail. I got talking with several of them. One, a yellow woman, told me she came from Culpepper. 'All your family with you?' 'All but one, Sir, my mistress sold one of my daughters down South, maybe three years ago.' 'What did she get for her?' 'Twelve hundred dollars: she was fourteen years old.' Does it not seem barbarous that this woman, who was no darker complexioned than many of our friends, should have a child sold off in that way? I did know already that Virginia used to depend much on the slave trade; but it comes more home to one when one hears viva voce from the mother herself of a case like this. The masters of all the slaves to whom I spoke today are in the rebel army.

Friday, October 2

I went first thing this morning to call on Mr. Seward. He is very accessible. But I was quite shocked by his appearance: he was so bowed. I was told afterwards that he has a son very ill just now with one of the armies. If I had known that before, I should not have gone. I told him of my having been in eastern Maryland. He told me that Government is directing the revolution there, that it was bound to happen some time and the sooner over the better. The photographs of Seward look quite different from how he really appears now. Public life in such emergencies as he has gone through must be desperately hard.

Yesterday I saw Mr. Lincoln drive past in his carriage and four – alone but followed by a guard of about fifty cavalry. He looks ordinary enough.

When I came in to breakfast I found General Martindale, who also lodges in this house. He was reading the paper and I asked him the news – from this beginning he entered into a dissertation on forms of Government. These political Generals are among American curiosities. This particular one admires England greatly. He considers it certain that when the rebellion is settled there will be a war to drive the French out of Mexico; but if the rebellion cannot be crushed, he sees no chance for Republican Government in America. It will be proved a failure and it will be followed by despotism. He is for no compromise with slavery. He is hopeful of crushing the rebels. He ridicules, as all here seem to do, the suggestion that Jeff. Davis will liberate the slaves. He believes that the negroes will fight well and understand perfectly what they are fighting for. 'What is your opinion?', said he, turning to the black servant who was keeping the flies off us with a feather brush as we breakfasted. The black man said

[98]

the slaves would not be such fools as to fight for Jeff. Davis. The fact is that the slaves are not such fools as they look.

I have just read a book called Under the Pines *by Edmund Kirke. It professes to be all true and I fancy most of it is. He discovered a sort of freemasonry and secret organization of slaves in South Carolina. From what I saw and heard in Maryland I can well believe it. Mr. Seward told me that there is a camp of six thousand freedmen on the other side of the Potomac and that I may have a pass to see it by applying to his son at the State Department.*

At Mr. Wise's I met Admiral Davis, chief of the Navy Department, and Assistant Secretary Fox — both striking men. Keep this letter for my journal: I write instead of journalizing.

SATURDAY, OCTOBER 3

Washington

At the Capitol yesterday. Saw rotunda with pictures of the surrender of Cornwallis, Burgoyne, etc. copied from the Newhaven Trumbulls. Saw the Senate House of brown marble from Tennessee and white marble from Massachusetts. Looked at the statuary on the east front and at the great bronze statue of Liberty, which is to crown the dome, now lying in pieces. She has a helmet on and a wreath in one hand. I was shown round by an Irishman who came from Carlow thirty-six years ago — a friend of the head gardener here.

SUNDAY, OCTOBER 4

Am writing on the heights overlooking the Potomac four miles south of Washington. Came out here yesterday with Wormley. Found Captain Frank

Yates Thompson's sketch of view from heights overlooking the Potomac River and Washington, D.C.

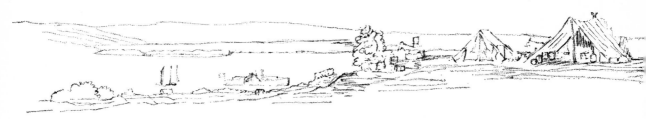

Sketch (from same viewpoint as preceding sketch) showing the camp beside the Potomac,
four miles below Washington.

Furness, Bill Treichel, 'Jake' Windsor, Charley Cox, Sage Clarke and others
of the 6th Cavalry regiment. As I write this, the scene before me is most striking.
The broad Potomac, muddy and blue by streaks as the light catches it, a strip of
flat land between the river and the bluff where I am seated, and beyond the river
the gently undulating Virginian shore dotted with white tents and United
States flags. Up the river and beyond the Eastern Branch, the Capitol and
Washington's monument with the city lying between them. Tents and hospital
ranges diversify the flat land above where I am sitting. Opposite me the land
is divided into fields of corn and grass. Single cavalry soldiers ride from time to
time along the roads. Steam tugs going between Washington and Alexandria
patrol the river, flags flying, whistles blowing. Just above me a column of cavalry
is descending the bluff, many white horses among them, making up a marvellous picture with the tents which peep through the trees behind them. I
hear the sound of men galloping along the road beneath.

THURSDAY, OCTOBER 8

Wheeling, Ohio

Now for an account of my journey from Washington. I left yesterday morning, Wormley's black announcing the carriage at 5.30 a.m. I had an hour before
the train left. Dressed in a hurry and was going to get my ticket at the depot
when a polite man with an air of mild and pitying authority told me to go by the
Baltimore and Ohio railroad — thirty-seven miles shorter than the Penn-Central
— quite safe, etc. He gave me a ticket to Cleveland for $13.50 and behold me
in the ladies' car to which he ushered me eating my two ham sandwiches carried
off from Wormley's. So to the relay house where, waiting for the cars from
Baltimore, I met Algernon Gilliat of London and Liverpool. He raised my bile
by having been with the army for three days at Meade's headquarters. His
impression is that there will be no fighting there.

Joined in the rail car by a native of Frederick on his way to Michigan, a
devoted Unionist with one son killed and another sick to death in the army.
At Frederick the Rebs. took all he had so that he was fain to borrow from a
scratch acquaintance, who had not been molested, some food for his family.
He now leaves Maryland at great sacrifice for the sake of a quiet life. Slavery

has long been destroyed in his part of Maryland; it was too near Pennsylvania. Two slaves of his ran away and asked to be taken back; he would not have them and released the rest. Gave me lunch of biscuits, gingerbread and tongue – a little grey-bearded man.

On we went crossing the Potomac on a skeleton bridge near the piers of a destroyed bridge, past Harper's Ferry where we saw the ruins of the hotel and the armoury where John Brown defended himself and was taken – a little one-storey building. On to Martinsburg. Talked with an old woman. She hoped the Rebs. would never come back to Maryland, her native place. 'Things in Maryland are just beginning to look up again.' Deserters from the Rebel army went past her house every morning. On to Oakland, all the way through hills along the Potomac valley in the rain. An Ohio soldier told me that he had been captured at Winchester and put in the Libbey prison. Described how the men cooked their dole of flour in tobacco-boxes or anything they could get. He now had chronic diarrhoea.

At Oakland had good supper with Gilliat and the landlord, a secessionist who owns two slaves, the only ones in Oakland. Next morning talked with secessionists in the bar-room. They said that I knew nothing about the negro. 'He will fight for his master with devotion' (what an absurd hallucination!). On from Oakland at about 9.00 a.m. – glades and wooded hillsides and rocky streams and log huts. Came onto the Ohio river about 4.00 p.m. flowing between wooded slopes. Passed pontoon bridge built for troops. Talked in the car with a Hopkinsville Kentuckian, named Red Durrett. He had been to Washington and now returns angry because he could not see his son in the Potomac army, his only son. Told me of his journey out and the alarm in the rail cars near Louisville. The guard asked for volunteers among the passengers: guerillas fired a bridge, but then ran. He supported abolition: 'But what do we do with the slaves?' He believes in colonization.

After a wash at the Maclure House hotel, Wheeling, sauntered down to the Spring Hotel on the river. Talked with boy at the hotel door and to a pay-master of the army and to Col. Jarry of the West Virginia Legislature. Col. Jarry is going to Kansas to look after land which he has bought there. He was in the Virginian Convention and departed after the ordinance of secession: there had been a telegraph from Richmond to seize him and his companions.

SATURDAY, OCTOBER 10

Detroit, Michigan

Red Durrett of Hopkinsville, Kentucky, was in the car again today. Told me how his town had been occupied by Morgan, whose men came in with Union shouts and in Federal uniform. The secessionists all ran away in fear and the troops made exactions from all who stayed. He asked to see Morgan at Columbus: he wanted to see how he looked with his head shaved, but he was not allowed.

Dined at Wellsville. Talked with James H. Nugent of Chicago, born in Ireland, a first lieutenant lately stationed at Petersburg. Regiment now reduced to 400 seasoned men under Col. Mulligan, 'the best officer in the army, kept only a Col. because of jealousy of foreigners'. My lieutenant is a tall handsome young fellow twenty years old, with long thick golden hair: going home for twenty days' leave, the first time he has been absent from duty since the War began. They have had hard work in West Virginia – many long marches: lost 250 killed and wounded at Lexington, Missouri. He was much disgusted by what I told him of the black troops I had seen. 'Did you say they were in uniform, Sir?' 'Yes.' 'Same as ours?' His look of disgust was worth seeing. I said they drilled well. He said that if they put any of them in West Virginia his men would 'drill them in a different fashion'. Prefers on long marches to lie without blanket rather than carry a blanket. This youth is an example of some of the benefits of war. Living all his life in Chicago, he was always at theatres, operas, etc.; and he thinks that he owes his good health while campaigning to his constitution having been accustomed to trial by staying up late in Chicago!! The war has developed him immensely, I guess.

Up to the Ohio valley past coal mines and quarries. Hills about the height of the Superga range opposite Turin. Turned across to Cleveland through a well-farmed flourishing country. Houses in New England style. At Alliance talked with a medalled officer of the Potomac army. Sat with Dr. Hildreth of Detroit, chief of eye and ear military hospital at Washington: an abolitionist, he would have spoken to Nugent if he hadn't heard him speak against black soldiers.

Took the boat at Cleveland, the *May Queen*, for Detroit, where stayed at the Russell House and called on Alex Macgraw and found him in his huge boot and shoe store. He took me a drive in the afternoon to see the Michigan copper works. He is an abolitionist: travels much to see the world, was recently in Moscow.

SUNDAY, OCTOBER 11

Ann Arbor, Michigan

Sat next to a New Yorker (Mr. Bates) at breakfast. 'Seems a pretty good hotel, Sir,' I said. 'Only been here one night, Sir, and can't judge,' was the reply.

Sauntered out after breakfast with Bates, who is here on business. He took the opportunity of looking at the signs of the shops. Had heard that there were some good men in his line at Ann Arbor. 'Well, Sir, there you see one: Paints and Oils and Medicines.' So we went round Ann Arbor together.

Went to a Methodist church with 'paints and oils': sermon was insufferable rant, as appeared also to Bates. 'Blood, blood, blood'; but the congregation seemed to think it good.

After dinner I walked out north in the clear air. Just out of town I overtook a tall, studious but well-made man with English whiskers, who turned out to be a student from Milwaukee and the son of a Scotchman who emigrated when he was seven years old from near Glasgow. He was going to England for a tour when war broke out. But at New York he heard about Fort Sumpter: he enlisted at once for nine months in a Pennsylvania regiment. Has a brother, his only one, with Rosecrans and has not heard of him since the battle of Chickamauga.

SUNDAY, OCTOBER 11

Letter to brother Sam

Ann Arbor

Please forward the enclosed letter to the Daily News. *Do you think they will publish it? It is a good story, is it not? I am on my way to Chicago and the West. It is splendid autumn weather, very hot by day and hard frosts by night. I stopped here on Sunday in order to visit the University — having been invited by a Professor to do so. But I found that my professor had turned politician and gone to New York to stand for the State Legislature. So I have had Sunday to myself and employed it to write the enclosed letter to the* Daily News. *I think I shall get home by the New Year.*

SUNDAY, OCTOBER 11

Letter to the *Daily News*

Ann Arbor

I have heard one story in Maryland which seems to me to illustrate very well two features of slavery. I was riding some twelve miles from Washington on the banks of the Potomac, and turned into a farm on the river's brink to enquire about shooting. It was an ordinary Maryland farm. As we approached the river, by its private lane, the farmhouse lay to the right, close to the water, and only a few feet above its level. To the left was the slave quarter with a negro woman and a mulatto child basking at the door. Three men sat on the verandah looking landwards, sheltered from the hot sun. To look at, they were perfect Southerners — especially one of them, a tall, lanky man of thirty or forty, with long straight hair, black eyes and a dark, un-wholesome complexion. After some talk about the reed-birds and ducks, the partridges and the blackbirds, I asked Mr. Macgruder, the farmer, how he was off for labour. He said he lost all his servants on June 19 last year — all except one, the woman I had seen. I asked him what would be the new system adopted now the niggers had gone. He did not know. I should say that he has scarcely any of his farm of 400 acres in tillage this year. As to white labour, it might perhaps be got, he said, when the war ended; but he had this objection to it — he 'could not bear to see a white man at work in his field'. 'Do you think, Sir, that a white man could ever hoe like a negro?' No, it seemed to him against nature.

I expressed wonder that the slaves were so ready to leave their master who in some cases must have been very kind to them. 'Ah, Sir, you don't know the ungrate-fulness of the negro. Why, some of my negroes rested far more than I do; they had plenty to eat and drink; their work, you may say, was nothing they could not do. But I'll give you an example. My father had a negro named George whom he used as a body-servant. One day, this negro got frost-bitten very badly, and my father, who was something of a doctor, saw how it was and went to him and said "Now, George, you're in a bad case. If your hands and feet are taken off, you may live, if not, you will die. Would you rather live without hands and feet, or die? It will be a great expense to me to have them cut off; but you have been a good servant and I'll have it done if you say the word."" George said the word and his hands and feet were cut off accordingly, 'at considerable expense'. 'Well, Sir, would you believe it, that negro has run away. After being kept useless and at some expense by my father, and afterwards by me, for more than thirty years (besides the expense of having his limbs cut off, of which you'd have thought he would have had some memory), he tried to get away last year when the others went. Well, I got him back and had him tied up, for I thought he must be mad. But it was no use, he got away again, and walked to Washington, and he's there now.' I asked how he could walk so far without feet. 'Oh, he just stumped along. He was always a right smart nigger, and he could do many things after he lost his limbs. He could attend to the cooking and sew with his teeth very well, and could get on a horse and ride as easy as look. He was always a remarkably strong nigger. Why, even after he lost his hands, he could kill a man, almost, with a blow of one of his knobs.'

So the white man sits in his tumble-down verandah, folding his hands and gazing on his untilled acres because he conceives that any life more active than an overseer's is incompatible with his white skin; and the mutilated old nigger so strongly yearns for liberty that he leaves cornbake and molasses and 'better clothes than I have, Sir,' to stump twelve miles to Washington that he may there starve but be free.

Here was supposed to be an instance of the 'ungratefulness' of the negro. To my mind it was an instance rather of that craving after freedom and selfownership which is one of the most hopeful characteristics of the slave population. Little did the Maryland farmer suspect, as he told me of this example of the ungratefulness of his negro, that he was himself a speaking example of that unconscious degradation of the white man under the curse of slavery which Jefferson foretold sixty years ago and which culminated in the Rebellion.

TUESDAY, OCTOBER 13

Chicago, Illinois

I left Ann Arbor at 9.00 a.m. yesterday in a commodious Michigan Central rail car. I sat beside a dyspeptic looking Colonel (First Michigan Cavalry) searching for recruits, finding none — 'people have lost their interest in the War: Vallandigham will be elected Governor of Ohio tomorrow', he said. 'I didn't believe it until I visited Columbus lately.' Columbus is in the heart of the copperhead part of the State of Ohio and Vallandigham represents the extreme peace and pro-South element in the Democratic Party.

At Dexter we stopped three hours owing to an accident — two freight cars off the line. Talked with Calvin Day of Hartford, Conn., a little, shaven, grey-haired man, a polished and travelled New Englander, who has property at Chicago — talkative and had never been west before. He has a picture of Terni by d'Azeglio,[7] was at Florence during the revolution of '59 and watched it from the Uffizi Gallery. A strong Republican. He told me a story of a hotel keeper in Florida who was going to whip one of his negro girls for stealing clothes: the Northern ladies in the house said they would call for their bill if he did: the girl was afterwards found to be innocent.

WEDNESDAY, OCTOBER 14

Chicago

At G. C. Clarke's. He lives with Mr. Goodwin and his wife. Mr. Goodwin is a lawyer, with his practice chiefly in the U.S. Federal Courts. At dinner was also Charles A. Gregory, an acute, hard-working New Englander of thirty, a lawyer with business mainly in the State Court. Goodwin is an exceedingly

7. Massimo Tapanelli Marchese d'Azeglio, 1798–1866, of Turin: Italian statesman and painter of landscapes.

scrubby little man (five feet four inches). He used to take exercise by gymnastics or walking; but now rolls on the floor with his child every evening, which accomplishes the same purpose. It seems Chicago is divided about half and half between the two parties in politics. About 10,000 votes polled on each side in the last contest. After dinner, Goodwin proposed billiards at his partner's house. We went and had some games.

Goodwin insisted on lighting up the drawing-room for my edification. The attractions were a brass or gilt chandelier adorned with chains and brass pendants. He thought I should be interested to see how they got up a drawing-room in Chicago. There was a French clock in the library, a snug little room, representing Napoleon burning a death-warrant and throwing it into the fire.

Newspaper cutting, Chicago.

FRIDAY, OCTOBER 16

Letter to mother

Milwaukee, Wisconsin

I got here today from Chicago and have been over a grain elevator and through a slaughter house and shall go tomorrow with a joyful heart. The elevators here and at Chicago are on a great scale. The slaughter houses are a disgusting spectacle. It must make a man quite brutal to kill two hundred oxen in a day. These ports on the lake send out meat and corn and take in lumber and salt, and the towns are simply collections of men attracted from all parts of the earth to carry on the business of the places where they settle. There are no 'natives' because when a man who is now forty was born there was only the howling prairie. The saving element is the New England element. I had a letter to one New Englander at Chicago, a young man teaching Latin at the High School. He introduced me to a couple of lawyers, both Eastern men. The clergy too are mostly Easterners.

The chief hope for the Western States lies in the school system which has been introduced from the East. I was much struck by the High School at Chicago. Boys and girls are taught together. There are about six hundred in the school who are selected from the grammar schools at the age of thirteen and stay four years. People here seem quite aware that with republican institutions safety lies in the diffusion of education. The schools are all free throughout the Northern States. I never saw such marks of interest and diligence in any pupils as I saw at Chicago. The only penalty is dismissal from the school and the only reward is the credit of a high place. It is wonderful how well the system seems to answer. The masters I spoke to approve very highly of teaching both sexes together; they say that the emulation consequent thereon is a valuable stimulus to both. There is no doubt but that it is a grand benefit to the girls as compared with our system and I am inclined to think it the natural way and ours the reverse. It never occurred to me why American women are on the whole so much more intellectual than English women till I heard a lot of girls do their latin in class with boys. It requires a woman in England to be very clever to get hold of the idea that ceteris paribus her mind is equal to a man's. Once throw boys and girls together in class and the stupidest girl can see it at once.

So you sympathize with the North, only 'they are so illiberal and overbearing towards others'. I think you are getting on very well.

SUNDAY, OCTOBER 18

Letter to sister Meggie written aboard 'The Northern Belle' tied to the wharf at La Crosse, Wisconsin

on the Mississippi

I am sitting in a long saloon at either end of which is a stove. A violent gale of raw and cold wind with rain is blowing outside and penetrates every part of the long saloon except perhaps the immediate neighbourhood of the stoves. Round one of the stoves, cowering, sit some twenty-five men. Round the other some twenty women with perhaps twelve children who are squalling in a way which is not unreasonable in their unhappy position. The whole of these people came onto the boat and into the saloon last night at ten o'clock having most of them come by rail cars from Milwaukee, which place they left at midday. They spent last night in cells along the sides of the saloon which are pleasantly called 'staterooms' each of which contains two shelves. I lay on a lower shelf and was going to sleep when an exceedingly stout man (I did not see how stout he was till morning or I should have been much more frightened) climbed into the upper shelf and I was roused by a fearful creaking and bulging of the board about 18 inches above my face. The danger seemed excessive but no harm was done. If ever I have nightmares they will take this form. We are told there is a chance of starting at about one o'clock today. I console myself with the reflection that the rain would make any place a disgusting prison on such a day as this and by reading Don Quixote who certainly gets into worse messes than I have.

You would think the men here great brutes. They seem to be mostly just miscellaneous poor people from all countries who have come out here to settle. 'Think of locating anywheres here, Sir?' is the question generally asked of me. 'Come with me fifty miles southwest of this and I'll show you a tract of splendid wheatgrowing country — as fine land as you would wish to see.'

THURSDAY, OCTOBER 22

Letter to father

Boat on the Mississippi: Prairie du Chien

I write this on board a steamer on my way down the river to St. Louis. My last letter to you was from Ann Arbor, Michigan. Since then I have visited Chicago and Milwaukee and spent three days at Winona in Minnesota. I intended to have gone from Winona by land to St. Paul with a view of seeing something of the newly settled wheat growing land there which is of immense extent and filling up rapidly; but it is getting very cold up here and there seems no immediate prospect of settled weather. So I took two days duck-shooting at Winona and left last night.

Travelling here is by no means luxurious just now. The war has a good deal disorganized the river traffic by absorbing the best boats. It is very cold too; and the scenery of brown bluffs on either side of the river, a leaden sky above and an occasional string of ducks or geese, is depressing to the mind of the traveller. All the towns I have visited seem to be thriving with lots of building going on and the wharves encumbered with traffic, railroads constructed, new land reclaimed, and every sign of activity.

Yesterday as I was waiting for duck in a swamp along the Mississippi five miles above Winona a man and dog came up and, after he had assisted me to get a few ducks which had fallen in the water, we finally walked back to town together. I mention him because he was so violent a Unionist. He talked about the blood of his murdered brothers, of whom he had had two killed in battle and one wounded and one a prisoner. They had been five in all and had drawn lots who should not go, and according to him that was the only reason he had not gone too. He had a very good dog and was a capital shot and would make a first-rate soldier.

These western people are to my mind the best material for soldiers possible. They live a rough-and-tumble sort of life anyhow, having lots of shooting and camping out a good deal in quest of it. The general feeling hereabouts seems to be quite as strong for the Union as in the East, though in mercantile towns like Chicago, Milwaukee, etc. there is a large foreign vote made up of Germans and Irish and English and Canadians who do not feel so strongly. On the way from Milwaukee to Winona I took the boat and experienced some of the discomforts of Mississippi travel. It was blowing a cold northerly gale when we got to La Crosse late on Saturday night. The boat ought to have gone at once but whether on account of the wind or to get more freight she did not leave till late on Sunday night; and the passengers, especially those that could not solace themselves with tobacco and expectoration, passed a melancholy day.

I fell in with one man there who interested me. He was a gaunt spectre of a man dressed in butternut serge and was on his way from North Carolina to Minnesota. By his own account he left his native state, because he was a Unionist, a year ago; but because of the War he could only get as far as eastern Tennessee from which region he was unable to get away till Burnside's recent advance put him within the Union lines. His wife gave me an illustration of the straits to which the War had reduced them in the South. They had not seen coffee for a long time, but drank what they called 'Jeff Coffee' being wheat or barley roasted and ground as if it were coffee. This, they say, is the prevailing beverage now in North Carolina and eastern Tennessee.

Mr. Everett is to deliver an address at the opening of the cemetery at Gettysburg on November the nineteenth which I should much like to hear.

TUESDAY, OCTOBER 27

St. Louis, Missouri

To Lindell House. Found letters a month old from Sam and Meg.
Called on Judge Krum. Found him at dinner; but he came out and talked. Says that in Missouri the Unionists are about equally divided between Jacobins

and Conservatives. The 'disunionists' laugh to see them fight; but they are a small minority now. St. Louis has suffered much from the stoppage of the river commerce and the passenger traffic between North and South.

At 7.30 p.m. went to hear Hackett as Falstaff in the St. Louis theatre. There was only very faint cheering after the two final lines:

Rebellion must be outdone.
Let us not stop till all that's lost be won.

There was an *attempt* to applaud, but the house must have been mainly secessionist. Falstaff was wonderful. Hackett is above seventy and has tried farming in Illinois; but now returns to acting.

THURSDAY, OCTOBER 29

I sallied out yesterday after breakfast and after spending some time at the reading-room where there was a pile of *The Times* up to October 10. I found the insolent tone of *The Times* towards this country had not at all abated.

I called about midday on Dr. Pope. He is a surgeon and is one of the few examples in this country of a surgeon who is not a general practitioner also. He lives in a capital house (corner of 10th and Locust) and invited me for a drive this afternoon at 4 p.m. He was in England in 1839. I took a stroll in the afternoon to the wharf and saw a line of steam-boats alongside in which were various goods almost all such as might come under the head of army stores. I sauntered along and, seeing a steamer marked New Orleans, was for going on board. I had just stepped on deck when a man told me it was forbidden to go aft and I learned from him that, since the burning of eight steamers here, a strict watch is kept and he is the watchman. He pointed also to the guard along the wharf. Private freight is, he told me, prohibited just now. Most of the boats are wanted for army supply. 'That pays very badly,' he said, 'as the government price is low; and this boat refuses to take government stores unless obliged.' Sailors get $45 a month going down the river. I went on and saw a monitor with one turret. I had now got to the south end of the shipping and turned back into the town, where I passed many German shops.

I got to Dr. Pope's in time. His two-horse hooded carriage was at the door and we drove out to Henry Shaw's garden. He had been given by the City a tract of land to be made into a garden with a horticultural college attached. He is an Englishman who made money in hardware. We got back to tea. Mr. Dox, brother-in-law of Dr. Pope, from Huntsville, Alabama, was there. Mrs. Pope is a violent Southerner. She heard from Huntsville in September that her friends there are in a sad state. They have no tea, coffee or sugar and able-bodied servants are all impressed or run away. Mr. Dox was born in New York State, and became a planter in Alabama. He despises the present Washington administration, and thinks that a Democratic government would have ended the War much sooner. Mrs. Pope wants to send her boy to Eton and wishes they were a colony again under England. It amused me to hear Mrs. Pope's abuse of the negro race — how she 'knew them, having been among them all her life', how 'they are deceitful and dishonest by nature'. 'The free negroes are less happy and less manageable than the slaves : you can control *them*.' This pro-Southern feeling among the women is often found in families where the men are Unionists.

A story occurs to me here, told me by Miss Chamberlayne at Oxford, Maryland. She corresponds with a Miss Hammond of New Jersey. Miss H. is abolitionist in her sympathies. Miss Chamberlayne wrote for a lock of her hair. Miss H. said her maid told her she could not spare one. This mention of the maid affected Miss C : 'Why, I certainly could never be happy to have my hair done by a white woman, making a slave of my own flesh and blood, as it were.'

I found Governor Hamilton R. Gamble's* office opposite the Court House, a domed Greek building in the middle of the town. I went up an office stair and at the top found a seedy soldier with a shabby dark-blue jacket and shabby light-blue trousers, a round back and sinister aspect. To him I gave my letter of introduction and my card. I found the Governor a hale man, with flyaway white hair and Palmerston whiskers, his right arm in a black sling and a cigar between very imperfect rows of teeth. He nodded after reading the letter, asked me how long I had been in St. Louis, whether I was going to remain and settle. He said there was room for all the population of England in this country. He advised me that Louisville was the place to get a pass for Chattanooga, which he thought a stranger would get easier than a citizen. When the war broke out, the Legislature of Missouri was for secession. A Convention was called, of which Gamble was a member, which was expected to carry the country out of the Union. It proved loyal, electing a new Legislature with Gamble as Governor.

I now went to Captain George D. Wise, Assistant Quartermaster, who is like his brother in Washington with a shrivelled face and stiff hair and beard. He had just finished his business and half-closed his office at St. Louis : he was finishing a letter to Admiral Davis when I came in. He introduced me to a Mr. Harrison, an ungainly but kindly man who mines at Iron Mountain. He said the iron there is the purest and strongest in the world. It goes as far as Pittsburgh to mix with weaker sorts. It is first-rate for the sides of ironclads.

FRIDAY, OCTOBER 30

Iron Mountain, Missouri

Yesterday at 6.00 p.m. I sallied forth again in a commencing shower, uncertain where to go. I rang the bell of Judge Krum. I found him sitting with his wife and daughter. On my saying that I should go and hear Hackett again tonight in *The Merry Wives* he volunteered to go with me. I had asked him about the Union Rally and he said it would be in the open air, but that there would be a really good one on Monday for which I had better wait. He has been fifteen years one of the directors of schools in St. Louis, managing funds and selecting teachers and the system is capital he thinks. In *The Merry Wives* Hackett was as good as before; but the comedy was too difficult for the others except for her who acted Mistress Ford.

Awakened this morning at five and got off most comfortably by rail car at 7.00 a.m. with Mr. Boyce, agent of the Harrison Shoto and Valley Company, which owns 26,000 acres all round the Iron Mountain – with three furnaces and rolling mills at St. Louis. I sat along with Boyce. Behind us were Mr. Dyer and Mr. King, the former a Jacobin farmer, the latter a car-wheel manufacturer of St. Louis going down about his iron supply. I asked Dyer what sort of men turned guerillas; 'No decent men, I suppose?' He said he did not know, and, lowering his voice: 'I say, no decent men, but I don't know that there may not be some sitting near me. That woman in mourning, sitting opposite, is sister of a well-known guerilla. I guess he must be dead, her being in black.' Soon after this he moved away, and Boyce eagerly explained to me how such men as Dyer were the ruin of the country. 'Now all he told you about people's throats being cut was a d——d lie.' Said Boyce turning to King, 'I am not sure he did not mean a hit at me when he said there might be guerillas sitting near'.

Arrived at Iron Mountain at 1.00 p.m. There were three inches of snow on the ground. I mushed through it to the hotel, a shed of a building which looked most unpromising. Boyce had gone on to his house without a word, so I thought I had better dine and see if the place was tenable till next day. I entered a beastly stove-heated common room and through it into a piazza behind the house, following which to the right I entered a rude dining-room where the walls were of whitewashed ill-fitting planks. I sat down in despair. Several men were gobbling. Soon some redeeming points appeared to me. The woman at the end was tidy-looking, the turkey was good, and so were the potatoes. I dined and asked about a room. The hostess showed me into one leading out of the piazza. So I put some of my things there and went out to look for Boyce. I went to his house, his store and his furnace, and finding him in none of these, was directed to a new furnace near which I found him with a

German foreman standing in the snow and wind. Walking down the hill back to my hotel I found an Irishman drawing dirty water from a well to boil some potatoes. I went with him to his cabin, a wooden hovel with pigs in it redeemed only by a good wood fire. Four men were playing cards and two sat by the fire. I sat also. One of them came from somewhere between Swineford and Ballina. He used to go to England for the harvest. They told me that all the unmarried Irish working here enlisted at the beginning of the war.

I came in at dark and the landlord, MacDonald, came to talk to me over tea. He and his wife have ten slaves. She said: 'We never had any trouble, but with one of them. He used to wait in the house and was a likely boy and very smart. Well he must needs have his freedom – it was two years ago – so he bought a knuckleduster and was for killing my husband ; but we found it out and sold him right off. We only got $700 for him, though.' She had been offered $2,000 for him and refused it just before. She is of Kentucky, from Shelbyville, and has many relations there. 'Some are on one side, some on the other. Bless you, it is the same about here, too,' she said. As to the slaves, 'Those that have mean masters have run away : the slaves of good masters have stayed.'

SATURDAY, OCTOBER 31

Breakfast on mackerel, pork chops and apple butter.

On paying my $1½ to Mr. MacDonald and telling him I should walk to Pilot Knob, he said he would go with me part way. 'You ride on horseback, I suppose, Sir?' So he went to saddle the horses and I lugged up my gun-case and valise and saw the two sorry nags equipped with Spanish pegged saddles. We sallied forth along the white and icy road. I had to bend down my hat-rim to avoid the glare as we faced the sun. Mr. M. was born in East Virginia.

Mr. Boyce said he had received a communication from the officer in command at Pilot Knob saying that if he and his people voted against the Government they would be regarded as enemies.

Mr. MacD. said he had two mules till lately, but sold them for safety. They were taken off by soldiers once ; but he got them back, knowing the General. Many people have had their animals carried off without payment. 'You see, Sir, one side takes what the other leaves, for they say "They wouldn't have left you that horse if you had not been friendly to them."' We emerged after two or three miles out of the wood onto Middlebrook, a small town. Here I left Mr. MacD. and continued walking along the single line of railway to Pilot Knob, which I ascended by a steep tramway used for descending the ore.

[113]

I had a fine view of the rocky top-valleys all round, rounded and wooded slopes and hills beyond them, the town to the West and houses scattered down the valley to the South and a small camp in the flat valley beyond the town.

I sat a few minutes on the top and then came down by a different tramway to the town in the valley. I entered a boarding house for dinner and dined well with a storekeeper who told me that parties of a hundred men could go as far as the Arkansas frontier and that parties of twenty-five men were safe enough anywhere round – but there would be danger for fewer.

SUNDAY, NOVEMBER 1

St. Louis

Breakfast at 8.30 a.m. and met my friend George Walker of Springfield, Mass. and his wife. We had a very cordial meeting. Their child died and they are touring for a month for the sake of Mrs. Walker's health.

I went with Judge Krum, who called for me, to the Unitarian Church, spacious and well arranged, and founded by New Englanders many of whom attend it now. Sermon by Mr. Ellis of Boston. To Judge Krum's for dinner at one o'clock. He had been in Washington lately. He knew Mr. Lincoln very well and Mary Anne and has often danced and ridden with her. She is always very kind to him at Washington. 'Mr. Lincoln is easily imposed upon; but when once he has found a man out, he knows how to deal with him better than any man.' K. thinks him the best politician the party has got, and 'not more honest than other men'. He lets Stanton bully him and compromises with him. 'If I were him, I'd kick Stanton out of the Cabinet.' He saw a good deal of Halleck.* 'General', he said to Halleck, 'what is your impression of the comparative merits of the two armies – Grant's men in the west or the Army of the Potomac?' Halleck said the 'six-footers' in the west always astonished him with their great bones and absence of fat. Western army discipline strikes an eastern soldier as loose. The officers discuss a movement with their men, pro and con. But when once it is ordered, they execute it with such vigour as if each man were fighting the whole battle. Krum said that Grant has the great merit of listening to all opinion and advice. He used to cart wood into St. Louis. 'He is untiring and thorough in all that he does.' Krum considers that the western armies are the backbone of the country. For five years he used to go on circuit in some counties of Illinois and Missouri and he described their well-to-do farmers as most hospitable. 'They are very hard to move, but when they do move they strike with force as this war shows.' Krum is of New York State and came west as a young man. He thinks the War is to last some time.

[114]

WEDNESDAY, NOVEMBER 4

Letter to mother

Lindell House, St. Louis

From now I go East again. I write this in the Mercantile Library of St. Louis. It is larger than the Athenaeum Library and the room is adorned with statues and pictures and is very quiet. I have had a good time here. Dr. Pope, to whom Henry Bright gave me a letter of introduction, has been very kind; also Judge Krum, a western lawyer whose wife is a sister of Mrs. White of Keene, with whom I spent a week in July. I also had a letter to Captain Wise who is here as one of the Quarter Masters for the Mississippi Fleet and is a brother-in-law of Mr. Everett's daughter. I had breakfast today with a man to whom Wilkins introduced me in the office of The Republican and who has been much in the South. He heard Jeff. Davis say in a speech 'ours is a predatory property and only by the lash can we retain it'. Captain Wise gave me a letter to General Robert Granger commanding at Nashville.

I saw an election here yesterday. It was conducted very quietly and ended in this city in favour of the abolitionists who want to end slavery in Missouri at once instead of waiting till 1870 as the present plan is. The North is getting on very fast with emancipation in its own limits.

THURSDAY, NOVEMBER 5

Letter to sister Meggie

Flora, Illinois

I set out from St. Louis with a ticket to Louisville which allowed me to stop anywhere on the road. I wanted to stop somewhere to shoot and see the country and quite by chance stopped at Flora about seventy miles from St. Louis. On landing from the rail car a German accosted me and asked me with great politeness to come with him. On arriving at his door I saw a lot of dogs lying round and soon found out that he is a noted hunter in these parts. His name is Eugen von Boeckmann and he comes from Stahlsund in northern Prussia and he is a remarkable character. His sitting-room is half-filled by an enormous piano, on which he and his wife play very well — which they should do, as he is a cousin of Flotow. It is curious that Martha *is my favourite opera and I appreciated the airs from it better than they would expect. What interests me about these people is that, though they keep a very small inn in a village of four hundred inhabitants in southern Illinois, they evidently were not at all low people in their own country. The wife especially is educated and refined and it seems*

[115]

odd to see a woman, who is well-read and accomplished and pretty, waiting on and cooking for travelling hucksters and blacksmiths. They were married in 1854 and went to London for their wedding tour. My host seems to devote himself mainly to shooting and we had a fine walk this afternoon after quail and rabbits and are going to make a long day tomorrow. This is the Indian summer here and today was a lovely summer's day, tho' the leaves are off the trees and the prairie grass all dry and brown. Looking round the horizon after dark one can see many fires on the prairie.

Eugen von Boeckmann. Sketch by Yates Thompson.

FRIDAY, NOVEMBER 6

You would like to have dined with me today. We were shooting all morning, Herr Boeckmann and I, and in the middle of the day we were ready for dinner. So we drove our buggy up to a small copse on the edge of the prairie and selected one prairie chicken and two quails which we proceeded to pluck. We sent the boy who drove our buggy to a farmhouse for bread and to fill our bucket with water. By the time that Herr B. had plucked and prepared the chicken I had plucked the two quails, an operation requiring much more skill than I had imagined. He had got a fire lighted of a few sticks and bits of bark and placed the three birds on his frying-pan. Having peppered and salted them and put some pieces of butter onto the pan he put a plate over all and set the pan on the fire. The sight was now very picturesque. He, I and the boy, a diminutive and loquacious youth of fifteen recently come here from New York (a grotesque example of perfect self-confidence) sat on the windward side of the fire, Herr B. assisting the gentle breeze by fanning the fire with his old wideawake. The two tired dogs lay basking and snoozing in the sun and the guns and the bucket of water with the yellow bread were the accessories in the scene of which the pan-covered fire was the centre. I can tell you that we enjoyed our bread and game and had a pleasant day altogether. We got seventeen chickens and five quails on the prairie and the cornfields and I shall stay for another day tomorrow.

SATURDAY, NOVEMBER 14

Continued from Louisville, Kentucky

I got here last night having stopped eight days at and near Flora. I was out hunting every day and am all the better for it. For four days we camped out about sixteen miles away from Flora on the edge of a prairie. The German who goes by the name of the mad Dutchman, or 'Chicken Charley' from the number of chickens which he kills, had a chill or fit of ague and had to lie in his tent all of one day. So I went out hunting alone and when I got back at dark, instead of finding him better as I had hoped and supper ready, I found him groaning in the tent and no fire, no water, nothing ready. Then came the terrible difficulty of collecting wood for a fire in the dark, cooking, etc. in all of which I may now be considered an adept. Happily next day quite by chance

Camping with von Boeckmann; sketch by Yates Thompson.

came our waggon and we got back to Flora. I came on here yesterday. I am going to Nashville tomorrow or next day.

P.S. There is a letter of mine in the Daily News *of October 17. Tell Sam to get it and have a look at it. They have not put my initials on it.*

SUNDAY, NOVEMBER 15

Louisville, Kentucky

Today made contact with U.S. Sanitary Commission. Called upon Dr. J. S. Newberry, who is in charge of the Western Department of the Commission, at his office at Fourth Street, between Chestnut and Broadway.

At tea at Galt House sat next to James E. Murdoch, an American actor just back from the front. He went there two months back to bury his son killed at Chickamauga. He stayed on as a volunteer helper. He had acted on the London stage in 1857. He stayed at Chattanooga and read a great deal to the wounded: he read 'The charge of the 600' on a hillside to some 2,000 men: their shouts after it and during it annoyed him.

He is an old man with long iron-grey hair and a short grey beard. I opened our conversation by remarking to him, when two young men at an adjoining table got up to go and took their crutches from a negro, that what first struck a stranger was the number of maimed men — these two had only two legs between them.

I hope to start for Nashville tomorrow. Wrote letter to The *Daily News*.

SUNDAY, NOVEMBER 15

Letter to the *Daily News*

Galt House, Louisville

On October 17 you printed a short account from me of negro recruiting in Maryland. Somebody has sent me a copy of the Morning Post *of October 13 containing a letter from Baltimore on the same day as mine. With Col. Burney organising*

Contemporary advertisement from a Louisville, Kentucky, newspaper.

two regiments of runaway slaves within a mile of where I was writing and the State about to vote the Radical ticket in the fall elections, this precious observer comes to the enlightened conclusion that 'the North is fighting for the extension of slavery and not for its extinction'. Possibly such as this may be good enough for the Morning Post. *I mention it to give vent to a little of the indignation aroused in me by the blind ignorance of what I may call the anti-liberal London press on all that concerns this country. Of course nothing that I can say will change their views. I should as soon expect a village clergyman to disbelieve in Noah's Ark. But when the Union has triumphed and the chief conspirators are domiciled at Paris or Havana, when cotton grown by free men cumbers the ports of the South and free schools are in all its villages and even eastern Virginia begins to smile again, then many people in England will see how blind they and their oracles have been.*

The struggle here is not so much between two nations as between two parties in one nation. There are numbers of Secessionists in the North and doubtless even still many Union men in the South. When peace is declared these men will go back. The abolition of slavery and of the three fifths[8] vote will take the wind out of the sails of the Southern aristocracy after the guerillas have been exterminated.

The contending parties in the Civil War in America on both sides are of English blood. Germans and Irish are mere accessories. The principals in the duel are Anglo-Saxon, and when once it is known who is the stronger the mass on the other side will acquiesce. The War must go on till the weaker party succumbs.

If ever a nation deserved to live it is the United States of America.

8. See note 1 2, page 55.

BOOK III

NOVEMBER 16 – DECEMBER 13

Editor's Introduction

To UNDERSTAND the strategy of the War it must be remembered that there were two distinct major campaigns in which the armies on both sides were under independent commanders responsible directly to their respective Presidents. These two campaigns were fought (1) between the Atlantic coast and the Alleghany Mountains and (2) between the Alleghany Mountains and the Mississippi River. All else was secondary.

In the first, the eastern theatre of the War, political and prestige considerations tended to influence military decisions. It contained the two capitals, Washington, D.C., and Richmond, Virginia, only 115 miles apart. Unionist armies had to be disposed in strength to defend Washington, and Richmond required the protection of the main Confederate army.

The chief battle area of the War was between and around Washington and Richmond. This was the campaigning ground of the Army of the Potomac, splendidly equipped and provisioned but for the first half of the War outmanoeuvred and outgeneralled by the smaller Army of Northern Virginia which was brilliantly led by General Robert E. Lee and his great lieutenant, General T. J. (Stonewall) Jackson who lost his life at Chancellorsville in May, 1863. After the Confederate victory at Chancellorsville, Lee went north to invade Pennsylvania. But he was stopped by the Army of the Potomac at Gettysburg on July 4, 1863, and forced to return south. Only six days before the Battle of Gettysburg, General George Meade had replaced General Joseph Hooker,* the defeated Unionist commander at Chancellorsville, as head of the Army of the Potomac. After Gettysburg there was a period of inaction in the eastern theatre of the War.

Meanwhile, on the same day as the Battle of Gettysburg, Vicksburg had surrendered to Grant. Until then the armies in the western theatre had been fighting for control of the great north–south communications link, the Mississippi River. Now they were to turn east.

It was in the western theatre that Grant made his name. His first major success was in February, 1862, when he forced the Confederate General Buckner to surrender Fort Donelson to him with 14,623 prisoners-of-war. Grant had insisted upon 'unconditional surrender', and Buckner had protested against such 'ungenerous and unchivalrous terms'. It has been suggested that this was in the mind of President Franklin D. Roosevelt when at the Casablanca Conference in 1943 he proposed 'unconditional surrender' as the terms for Germany and Japan.[1]

The fall of Fort Donelson in February 1862 brought about the immediate withdrawal of the Confederate troops from Nashville, the State capital of Tennessee, which they had held since September 1861. Grant was prevented by inter-command rivalries from occupying Nashville. Instead, General Buell,* who was directly responsible to Washington, sent two of his divisions there from the Army of the Cumberland.

In the western theatre of the War, the chain of command was unsatisfactory and confused. At the time of Fort Donelson, Grant was serving unhappily under General Halleck, a poor field commander, over-cautious and jealous of his authority. Halleck was recalled in July 1862 to Washington and Grant was then given command of two of the western armies, the Army of the Tennessee and the Army of the Mississippi. In October 1863, when he was still at Vicksburg, he received a summons from Lincoln to come to the rescue in a dangerous situation that had arisen at Chattanooga. He was then given command of all the Unionist armies in the Military Division of the Mississippi. Now for the first time a unified command was established for the whole western theatre between the Alleghanies and the Mississippi.

On October 17, Grant met Edwin M. Stanton, Secretary of War, at Louisville, Kentucky, and it was agreed that he would change the command of the Army of the Cumberland, now besieged in Chattanooga, by replacing the demoralized General Rosecrans by General George Thomas whose steadfastness at the Battle of Chickamauga had prevented defeat from becoming disaster. Grant then put his favourite General, William T. Sherman, at the head of the Army of the Tennessee which was under orders to march to Chattanooga from Memphis, 250 miles away in western Tennessee. General Hooker was ordered at the same time to bring two divisions to Chattanooga from the Army of the Potomac by a roundabout rail journey from Virginia.

Grant arrived in Chattanooga on October 23 and with his usual energy transformed the situation. As reinforcements came up, he made his plans and

1. From *Grant as Military Commander* by General Sir Charles Marshall-Cornwall, 1970.

dispositions and got ready to attack the strong positions held by the Confederate army commanded by General Braxton Bragg.

All this time Yates Thompson had been dallying and loitering on his way to Louisville. With my eye on the military developments so quickly taking shape in the Tennessee theatre, and in the knowledge that the great battle of Chattanooga would be joined on November 23, I read with some impatience the account in his Diary of eight early November days wasted between St. Louis and Louisville in the pursuit of quail and prairie chickens in the company of an eccentric German acquaintance.

At this point it is well to read about the sequence of events leading to the

Major-General William S. Rosecrans (courtesy of the National Archives).

Battle of Chattanooga by turning to the lecture given by Yates Thompson to the boys of Harrow School on March 7, 1865:

'On New Year's Day 1863 and for several days on each side of it there was fought the Battle of Murfreesboro thirty miles south of Nashville in which the Unionist General Rosecrans beat General Bragg. There was now a short lull — but in September General Rosecrans marched south from Murfreesboro to Chattanooga and was already in Georgia when he was furiously assailed by Generals Bragg and Longstreet and driven back to

Chattanooga with the loss of 15,000 men. After this defeat, Lincoln put at the head of the whole western armies of the Union the hero of Fort Donelson, Shiloh[2] and Vicksburg, the redoubtable General Grant.

And in what state did General Grant find the army in Chattanooga? He found it lying cowed and dispirited by its defeat, besieged by General Bragg's victorious army, with no means of communication northwards except one waggon track of forty weary miles, now deep in autumn mud, crossing the mountains from Chattanooga to Bridgeport. General Grant's first care was to mend the communications. His base of supply was Nashville. From Nashville, he controlled the railway for 120 miles as far as Bridgeport on the river Tennessee — his difficulty came in the journey from Bridgeport to Chattanooga, the railway and the river being commanded by the Confederate troops in Lookout Valley.

On my visit to the army, I travelled from Nashville along the railway in a train of hospital cars going south under the command of a surgeon to wait at Bridgeport for their freight of wounded soldiers to be carried back to the Nashville hospitals. At Bridgeport, I slept on Friday, November 20, and went on next day to Chattanooga by the new communications line which General Grant had opened to take the place of the 40 mile waggon track across the mountains.'

Bruce Catton writes: 'Chattanooga, from first to last, was the most completely theatrical battle of the whole War. It stirred Grant himself, who wrote to a friend: "The specticle was grand beyond anything that has been, or is likely to be, on this Continent. It is the first battle I have ever seen where a plan could be followed and from one place the field be within one view". As usual Grant was careless about his spelling; but the fearful pageantry of this battle got under his skin.'[3]

I have myself seen the battlefield and I have stood at the top of Lookout Mountain in the mist and the rain as it must have been on the second day when Hooker's men scaled the heights. I have heard the story told by my great-uncle as he recorded it each evening in his Diary at Chattanooga; and I can well understand what an unforgettable experience it must have been. He wrote down what he saw as it happened; and he put the pieces together from his conversations with the other observers whom he met on the battlefield. His Diary gives a coherent and accurate account of the Battle of Chattanooga. A few gaps need to be filled in and this can best be done by quoting some extracts from the records kept by two men who were also present and who saw everything from

2. The Battle of Shiloh, April 1862, is also known as Pittsburg Landing.
3. From *Grant Takes Command* by Bruce Catton, 1968.

the same vantage point, Fort Wood,[4] on the first two days of the battle, and from Orchard Knob, not far away, on the third day. These two observers were General M. C. Meigs, Quartermaster-General of the United States, visiting Grant's headquarters from Washington, and General Ulysses S. Grant himself.

General Meigs telegraphed an 'unofficial dispatch' to Washington on November 26 addressed to E. M. Stanton, Secretary of War. A copy was among my great-uncle's papers.

'On the 23rd at $11\frac{1}{2}$ A.M. General Grant ordered a demonstration against Mission Ridge. The troops marched out, formed in order, advanced in line of battle, as if on parade. The rebels watched the movement and formations from the summit of Mission Ridge, five hundred feet above us, and thought it was a review. It was a surprise in open daylight. At 3.00 P.M. the important advanced position of Orchard Knob and the lines right and left of it were in our possession.

'The next day [*November 24*] at daylight, General Sherman had five thousand men across the Tennessee established on its south bank. By midnight he had seized the extremity of Mission Ridge [*the Confederate right flank*]. General Howard,[5] with a brigade, opened communication with him from Chattanooga. General Hooker scaled the slopes of Lookout Mountain from the valley of Lookout Creek and established himself high on the mountain side in full view of Chattanooga. This raised the blockade and steamers were ordered from Bridgeport [*right through*] to Chattanooga.

'General Grant's headquarters during the afternoon of the 23rd and the day of the 24th were in Wood's redoubt.

'At daylight on the 25th the Stars and Stripes were discerned on the peak of Lookout. Hooker moved to the Rossville gap to strike Mission Ridge [*the Confederate left flank*]. The rebel troops were seen streaming along the narrow summit of Mission Ridge, concentrating on their right to overwhelm Sherman. Shot and shell screamed from Orchard Knob to Mission Ridge, and from Wood's redoubt over the heads of General Grant and General Thomas who were with us from where the whole could be seen as in an amphitheatre. Sherman sent an assault against Bragg's right. It was gallantly made, reached the edge of the crest, held its ground for what seemed to me an hour, but was then bloodily repulsed by reserves.

4. Fort Wood was named after General Wood of the Army of the Cumberland which was commanded by General Thomas. Generals Wood and Sheridan led their divisions to the summit of Missionary Ridge in the final assault on November 25.

5. Howard commanded a brigade in the force Hooker had brought to Chattanooga from the Army of the Potomac in Virginia.

'A general advance was then ordered at the signal of six cannon shots from Orchard Knob. We saw the rebels swarm out of their rifle pits and spread over the base of the ridge. Some regiments pressed on up the steep sides of the ridge. Here and there a colour was advanced beyond the line. The advance was supported and the whole line ordered to storm the heights. With cheers answering cheers the men swarmed upwards. Colour after colour was planted on the summit.

'Bragg left the house in which he had held his headquarters and rode to the rear as our troops crowded the hill on each side of him. General Grant proceeded to the summit. Hooker coming in from Rossville swept the right of the ridge and captured many prisoners. The Battle of Chattanooga was won and another victory added to the chaplet of Unconditional Surrender Grant.'

In 1885 Grant, aged 63, having served two terms as President of the United States, was dying of cancer and he was in debt. With dogged courage he completed the two volumes of his 'Personal Memoirs' four days before his death. They brought $450,000 to his family, more money than he had earned in his whole life-time. Professor Morison[6] in his Oxford lecture called them 'the greatest military memoirs since Caesar's'. But the two works were totally dissimilar in style and purpose and in their mode of compilation. Grant's memoirs show him as a man both simple and generous, just and honourable; and his admirable character shines through every page.

This was his plan for the Battle of Chattanooga:

'Sherman to attack the enemy's right flank . . . Hooker to perform a like service on our right . . . Thomas with the Army of the Cumberland at the centre was to assault while the enemy was engaged with most of his forces on his two flanks.' [Sherman arrived late.] 'By November 20 Sherman himself was at Brown's Ferry with the head of a column, but many of his troops were far behind.[7] So Thomas attacked first on the 23rd and Sherman only got his troops across the Tennessee to attack the northern end of Missionary Ridge on the 24th.'

On the evening of November 24 Grant telegraphed to President Lincoln: 'The fight today progressed favourably. Sherman carried the end of Missionary Ridge. Troops from Lookout Valley carried the point of the mountain. Hooker

6. Professor S. E. Morison (see page 15).

7. Sherman's army had marched 250 miles from Memphis in west Tennessee. Yates Thompson heard the last units crossing the Tennessee River at Bridgeport during the night of November 20.

reports two thousand prisoners taken.' Lincoln replied: 'Well done. Many thanks to all. Remember Burnside.'8

The stage was now set for the final attack on November 25. Grant in his Memoirs describes how, Hooker's attack on Bragg's left flank being delayed and Sherman hard pressed, he ordered Thomas to assault Missionary Ridge:

'The centre was where Thomas and I stood together [*on Orchard Knob*]. Our men drove the troops in front of them so closely that rebel and Union troops went over the first line of works almost at the same time. Without awaiting further orders or stopping to reform, on our troops went, over the second line of works and on for the crest.

'In the Battle of Chattanooga troops from the Army of the Potomac, from the Army of the Tennessee and the Army of the Cumberland participated. There was no jealousy, hardly rivalry. In this battle the Union Army numbered in round figures about sixty thousand men. We lost a little over seven hundred killed and four thousand eight hundred and fifty wounded and missing. The rebel loss was much greater in the aggregate, as we captured and sent north over six thousand one hundred prisoners.'

This was one of the least sanguinary, as well as the most complete, of all Grant's victories.

After the battle was won Grant sent Sherman north to relieve Burnside at Knoxville. Longstreet abandoned the siege of Knoxville when he heard that Sherman was on the way.

Grant summed up:

'Knoxville was now relieved; the anxiety of the President was relieved; the loyal population of the North rejoiced over the double victory – the raising of the siege of Knoxville and the victory of Chattanooga.'9

8. On November 4 the Confederate General, Longstreet, was ordered to leave Lookout Valley and take his army of 20,000 to besiege General Burnside who was at Knoxville with a small force. This altered the balance between the contending armies at Chattanooga, Bragg being reduced from 53,000 to 33,000 against Grant's 60,000. Grant was asked later whether he thought this had been a serious tactical error on Bragg's part. Grant said this was so, and on it being suggested that Bragg doubtless thought his position on Missionary Ridge was impregnable Grant replied: 'Well it *was* impregnable.'
9. 'Chattanooga was perhaps Grant's greatest tactical victory. He had taken over command of an army which was not only defeated, demoralized and starving, but also occupied a tactically impossible position. Yet within a month he had reorganized it, restored its morale and led it to victory.
'By his successive victories at Vicksburg and Chattanooga he had destroyed the two main nerve centres of Confederate resistance in the western theatre.' (From *Grant as Military Commander* by General Sir James Marshall-Cornwall, 1970.)
'Unquestionably this was one of the decisive engagements of the War. Grant dominated the

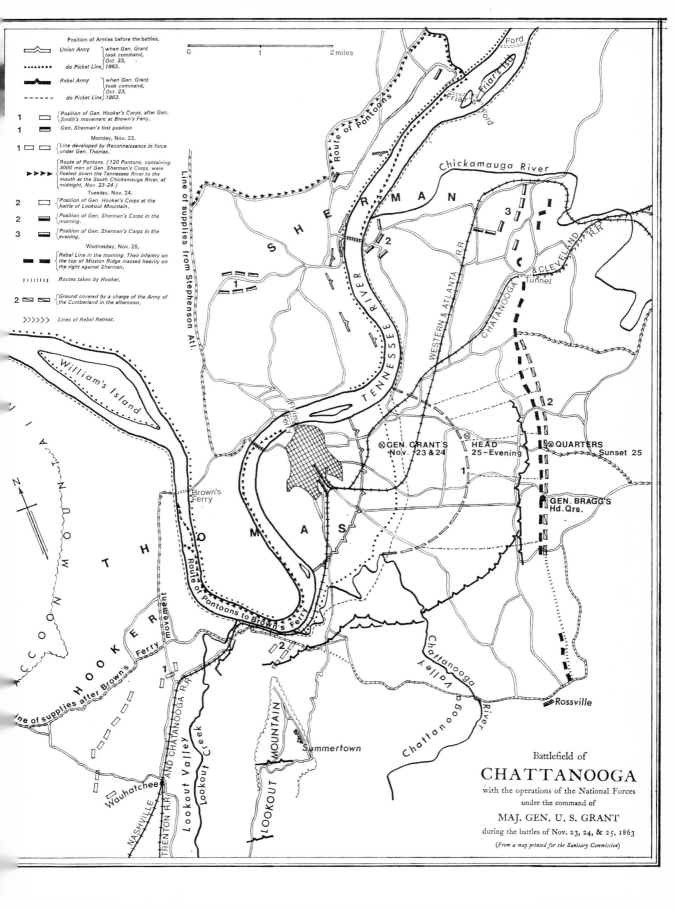

Battlefield of
CHATTANOOGA
with the operations of the National Forces
under the command of
MAJ. GEN. U. S. GRANT
during the battles of Nov. 23, 24, & 25, 1863

(From a map printed for the Sanitary Commission)

But the consequences of the Battle of Chattanooga went further than this. Lincoln now decided to establish in the field a single unified command over all the armies of the Union. At last he had found his man. Grant had finally proved himself at Chattanooga. As yet Lincoln had never met Grant. But when people criticized him he would say: 'I can't spare this General; he fights.' And so in March 1864 a special Act of Congress was passed enabling the President to make Grant the only ranking Lieutenant-General in the United States Army. From then onwards Grant, as General-in-Chief of all the armies of the United States, directed the twin campaigns, in the east and in the west, which brought final victory to the Union.

On the other side, Robert E. Lee was appointed General-in-Chief of the Confederate armies only at the eleventh hour, in February 1865. On April 9 he surrendered to Grant after the fall of Richmond at Appomattox Court House in Virginia.

On November 24, 1863 on Fort Wood my great-uncle watched General Grant directing the battle and he was filled with wonder and admiration. In his Diary that same evening he described Grant as 'the model of a modest and homely but efficient Yankee General'. He judged well.

Grant as a field commander stands above all the other generals on both sides who reached high command in the American Civil War – and some were remarkable men. He takes his place with some of the great military leaders of history. He had a clear mind; he made his plans and he carried them through with indestructible courage and tenacity. These qualities were combined with an unusually attractive character which inspired a devotion that was almost touching among some of his lieutenants. It is said that his simplicity and his loyalty to friends became faults in his later career when he was President of the United States. But it is rare to find a great military leader, and a tough fighter, endowed in such a high degree with the qualities of modesty and kindness, generosity and human understanding.

battlefield from beginning to end, he did just about what he intended to do before the first shot was fired and a postwar comment of Sherman's was largely justified: "It was a great victory – the neatest and cleanest battle I was ever in, and Grant deserves the credit of it all."' (From *Grant Takes Command* by Bruce Catton, 1968.)

The Diary

NOVEMBER 16 – DECEMBER 13

MONDAY, NOVEMBER 16

Nashville, Tennessee,
St. Clair Hotel, 9 P.M.

Up at five this morning at Louisville. Breakfasted with a man just back from the front who has been engaged on the Nashville Bridgeport railway: he says it is in a frightful state. Went by omnibus in the half light with some officers to the depot. Talked with a man from the Indiana Ohio border, a captain who was in an action in 1862 at Franklin near Nashville.

On the rail journey today from Louisville to Nashville we passed over a number of precipitous embankments. Two stations beyond Munfordville I

HEADQUARTERS UNITED STATES FORCES
Nashville, Nov. 15, 1863.

GENERAL ORDER NO. 43.

I. The Chief Quartermaster Department of the Cumberland, having stated that large quantities of corn in Montgomery, Stewart, Robertson and Cheatham counties, are being consumed by the distilleries, and that the same is absolutely necessary for the public service. The distilleries in these counties are hereby ordered to be closed.

By order of Brigadier-General R. S. Granger.   W. NEVIN,
Capt. and Ass't Adj't General.

nov15—1w

Cutting from Nashville newspaper.

saw a notice of the sale by auction of an estate — the terms for which the slaves were to be arranged on the day of the sale because they were 'rented or hired out'.

Talked with a boy soldier who told me about Colonel Wood[1] who was living in Munfordville. He said the troops at Munfordville lately caught some runaway slaves and returned them to their masters.

For the final two hours of the journey the landscape was more cultivated and I saw from the train planters' houses and the slaves' quarters. Most of the houses were tumbled down old houses. I saw, however, one or two large brick

1. The same Colonel Wood whom Yates Thompson had met in the train travelling from Canada to Syracuse (N.Y.) on August 29.

houses being built such as would be unknown in country districts further north. Crossed the Cumberland River into Nashville at about five o'clock in the afternoon. I set out for the rooms of the Sanitary Commission; but the omnibus by mistake left me by the offices of the U.S. Christian Commission. So I walked on past the Court House to the long storehouse of the Sanitary Commission and on to their rooms. On the way I met a dozen negroes shouting and yahyahing down the street. Asking a man on guard what was happening I was told: 'I guess they feel good. They have just been paid off.' At the Sanitary Commission I found some six or eight doctors and others with whom I had tea – an overworked lot. I came back to the hotel at eight o'clock. In the car the conductor, a seedy cad, cried out to some negroes wanting places: 'Now you black boys move out: you'll find plenty of room in the front cars' – then *sotto voce*: 'This is for white folks.' A refined looking officer in front of me pointed to some vacant seats by him for some negresses.

TUESDAY, NOVEMBER 17

Nashville

I have a good morning's work to recount: I went out at about 9.30 a.m. in search of Dr. J. B. Lindsley,* Chancellor of the University of Nashville. I went down to the steep river bank where quite a crowd of steamers were jostling one another, negroes lounging about, ambulance waggons with teams of mules, soldiers on foot and on horseback, steam blowing off, barrels rolling, sacks being shifted – and so on. An oldish man coming out of a cottage offered to direct me to the University – so we went south-east together. Two boys lounging at one of the college doors told us Dr. Lindsley would be there at ten – so I said I would go on to his house. The oldish man accompanied me again and we arrived on an open space where he showed me Dr. Lindsley's house – a one-storey building looking bright and cheerful. A black girl of eight or ten opened the door and told me Dr. L. was in town. So I asked for Mrs. Lindsley. She was very civil and told me much that interested me. Dr. Lindsley is of Rhode Island by birth and in the present troubles claims to emulate Bishop Juxon's[2] conduct as described by Clarendon. He devotes himself to his university pupils. He lectures on medicine: his reading is history and philosophy. Mrs. Lindsley's father comes from Virginia. She was born here. She had a brother shot through

2. Like Bishop Juxon in the period of the English Civil War, Lindsley kept the confidence of both sides. Juxon was Lord High Treasurer to Charles I; after the Restoration he became Archbishop of Canterbury under Charles II. It was said of him 'he made no enemies'.

the head fighting in Missouri, a Confederate colonel of a Tennessee regiment. She told me how early this year General Mitchell made them all take the oath of allegiance on pain of being sent south and how, after some hesitation, she went up to the Capitol and took it. She feels bound by it; but she thinks many took it as a form. I asked her about the slaves. She says they go off if they want to and nobody takes any steps to recover them. She sees numbers of them about the streets and thinks they may have a hard time of it this winter.

Soldiers visit the plantations and carry off slaves bodily to Nashville. She told me how one of her own girls had gone off: 'I came into the dining room one morning and found no cloth laid for breakfast. Where was Fanny? We could not find her in the house: so we went to look for her in her room in a small cottage where our servants live. She had gone and taken everything with her – the room was quite bare, bedstead, furniture, clothes, everything gone. Well, I said, I have been caught at last – for my friends had all been joking me that this would happen to me, as it had to them, and I never believed them, thinking I would have some suspicion first.' Mrs. L. told me the town had been dead when the War began. But it has now had a new start. Some Northern families are settling in, several stores have opened and it is very difficult to find a house. She has seen cotton for sale – showing that the laws against commerce have been relaxed. She told me Dr. L. was in the town on business and was to be found at an address in Cherry Street. So I went back down town again.

I found Dr. Lindsley to be a very small, sharp-featured man with a bad complexion and a scraggy black beard. He wore black clothes and a very dirty white collar. He walked me through the city first of all to call on Dr. Thurston, Medical Director of the Department, who would be able to introduce me to General Granger. He was not in – so we continued to the Capitol. On the way we passed an open space where were congregated some fifty or sixty men in various faded shades of butternut. Dr. L. said they were Confederate prisoners and we asked one of the guards, a smart young fellow from Michigan, about them. He said they were from Chattanooga and would many of them take the oath: some would probably enlist for the Union.

Only one of the prisoners had a uniform, an artillery man in a buff jacket with red facings: the mass of the Rebels in the West fight in their common clothes. The guard testified to the friendliness between Rebels and Unionists. Several of the prisoners were wounded, some were sick and all were as dirty and picturesquely clothed as a group of Italian beggars.

We went on to the Capitol, a regular Greek building of hard limestone from a quarry in sight. Here Secession had been decreed by what Dr. Lindsley described as a conspiracy. The Legislature voted for a Convention to settle the matter. The calling of the Convention was refused by a majority of 12,000 votes.

[136]

A Decree of Separation was then carried by the State Legislature in secret session.[3]

We went to the Senate House, where a committee was sitting to assess claims for destruction of property, etc. Its duties were to ascertain the loyalty of aggrieved persons and the value of the property destroyed. The view from the portico is very fine; but the suburbs are ravaged by the army camps.

We next went down another street towards my hotel and, seeing President Polk's old house with his tomb in the garden, went in to the garden to read the inscription:

'President 1845–49'

(he died in June 1849 after his term was over). Dr. Lindsley took me into the house to call on Mrs. Polk – a well preserved lady whose conversation was most interesting. She had lived a long time in Washington and knew Calhoun intimately. At the time of Lincoln's election she was in Missouri and said to a gentleman who had been pressing to see her that she was a 'submissionist' as those in the South were called who were for opposition through the ballot and legal means alone. 'The gentleman drew back amazed and disgusted', she said. She greatly blames the chief men of the Democratic Party for the war because they divided their forces in the 1860 election instead of following one man as they should have done. She often goes to Murfreesboro and says that since that battle it has been a scene of desolation, not a fence, scarcely a tree, standing. She told me, as a piece of secret history known to few, that Mr. Calhoun had wanted to continue in office under her husband. When he came to bid her farewell she had said she hoped he would go to England as Minister. But he was for staying and working for the South. She said he was a charming man and a great talker. She 'messed' with him for three years in Washington – at that time the politicians used to club together for their meals.

It is a splendid Indian summer day. Dr. L. and I found Dr. Thurston at 24 Cherry Street and he went with us to Brigadier-General Granger. He was out – so I made an appointment for tomorrow morning. We walked on down to the river where the lime rock is exposed on the bluff. The rise of the Cumberland river must be enormous in the spring. We saw part of a ruined bridge which Sidney Johnstone* had destroyed when he went with 10,000 men to join Beauregard* at Shiloh. Buell followed and just arrived in time to save Grant.

3. The practice normally followed, if important constitutional matters are to be decided, is for the Governor of the State and the Legislature to propose a Constitutional Convention. Such a Convention in South Carolina voted the State out of the Union on December 17, 1860, after Lincoln had been elected President. It appears that in the present case the voters of Tennessee defeated the request for a Convention and that the Legislature then pushed through secession by secretly voting a 'Decree of Separation'.

The other bridge was also destroyed and is now replaced by a huge swinging bridge revolving on a pier in the middle of the river. We went to a place where we got good laager beer and then on to Reid's cotton storehouse – about 3,000 bales of cotton are to come into Nashville this year : there used to come about 15,000 bales.

Went to a wine party last night where there was a young lady from Dixie – also some Federal officers. She sang with chorus : 'Here's to Kentucky.' Then she gave 'Old Abe' a slam and sung : 'Here's to Jeff. Davis : he and God shall save us.' The Feds. laughed a good deal and one said he would drink to the last if God only were included.

We now went up to the University Hall for tea. Miss McGavock was there, a sister of Mrs. Lindsley. When the Rebs. were in Nashville she went for a visit to Columbus, Missouri. The Feds. advanced, and she was caught. She returned to Nashville two months ago, taking a month on the journey by way of Mobile, Montgomery, Atlanta and Huntsville – part way in an ambulance which broke down and then in a waggon without springs. She said the people in Columbus had tea, but very little coffee. I asked her if there were any Union men in Columbus. She said some were suspected ; but none dared say anything since feeling ran high.

WEDNESDAY, NOVEMBER 18

Nashville

I was up late. Sallied forth into Cherry Street after breakfast and entered what looked like a news room, with newspapers on stands at each side as you entered, writing desks and shelves lined with books. This is run by a soldiers' aid society, 'Christian Commission' by name. It was full of men reading and writing.

I went into a good haberdasher's and bought some handkerchiefs at fifteen cents apiece. The shop had been established for six years. I was told things were mending fast in Nashville. In the last three months goods have come down more easily from Louisville. When the Confederate army was only twenty or thirty miles from the town, goods had been held back because of the risk of smuggling from Nashville into Dixie.

I now called at the Sanitary Commission and found Dr. Read there. Dr. Newberry is to arrive tonight from Louisville. Then I went to General Granger's. Went straight upstairs into a large room where the General was seated in a corner of the room by the window – a military looking man, like an Austrian officer with a reddish face and heavy light coloured moustache. On one side of him was standing a 'butternut' under examination. On the other side of the General was a captain stating what he knew about the prisoner and the 'butternut' explaining that he was a Unionist to the core in a rich Irish brogue. The General read my letters of introduction and said: 'From Wise, eh!' I told him my wishes and he said: 'Captain, telegraph to General Thomas that an English gentleman with letters from my relations wants to go to the front.' He told us to come at eight o'clock to enquire for the result.

Went for a drink with Dr. Thurston. His office is in the house of a secessionist. I got a pass from him to visit the Cumberland Field Hospital: found it a collection of large tents, holding ten in each, covering a large area. I was tired and laid down on the planking of a tent that is to be beside a sick Indiana soldier

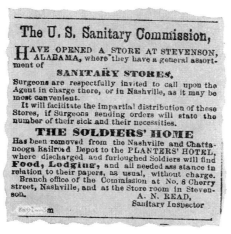

The U. S. Sanitary Commission,

HAVE OPENED A STORE AT STEVENSON, ALABAMA, where they have a general assortment of

SANITARY STORES,

Surgeons are respectfully invited to call upon the Agent in charge there, or in Nashville, as it may be most convenient.

It will facilitate the impartial distribution of these Stores, if Surgeons sending orders will state the number of their sick and their necessities.

THE SOLDIERS' HOME

Has been removed from the Nashville and Chattanooga Railroad Depot to the PLANTERS' HOTEL, where discharged and furloughed Soldiers will find **Food, Lodging,** and all needed assistance in relation to their papers, as usual, without charge.

Branch office of the Commission at No. 8 Cherry street, Nashville, and at the Store room in Stevenson.

A. N. READ,
Sanitary Inspector

Cutting from Nashville newspaper.

and contemplated the sunny view looking south-west. There were tents at various points in the undulating view. A load of hay passed in the distance and the Indiana soldier said it reminded him of home. Cattle were grazing on the trodden out land. I gave the Indiana soldier a newspaper. Then I had a talk with two convalescents, one of them wounded at Chickamauga. Walked back, dined and went at three o'clock to Dr. Lindsley's.

We walked out and sat on a charred trunk overlooking the river with the city in full view and the tower of the Capitol visible above the houses. We spoke of my projected trip to the front.

Dr. L. used to get $5,000 a year as Chancellor of the University; but, now that there is no State Government functioning here, he gets it not. Governor Andrew Johnson is 'Military Governor', like a proconsul. The Bank of Tennessee is somewhere down in Georgia. We went down by the reservoir; and

Dr. Lindsley gave me two books as mementoes and showed me the devastation of his garden with the angle of a rifle trench wedged into the middle of it. His

us of the American Watch Company,
182 BROADWAY, N. Y.

American Card Company's
New Union Playing Cards.
National Emblems.

Colonel of Eagles·

The suits are EAGLES, SHIELDS, STARS, and FLAGS. Colonel in place of King; Goddess of Liberty for Queen; Major for Jack.

The Union Playing Cards are the first and only genuine American Cards ever produced, and as they are entered according to Act of Congress, they can be manufactured only by the American Card Company.

The Cards are rapidly taking the place of Cards bearing Foreign emblems. The demand for them is unprecedented in the Card Trade, and they will soon become the Leading Card in the American market.

In playing with these Cards, they are to be called by the names the emblems represent, and as the emblems are as familiar as household words everywhere among the people of the American Republic, they can be used as readily the first occasion as cards bearing Foreign emblems.

The Union Cards are the most pleasing and attractive card ever made. They are produced in the highest style of the art, and each pack is put up in an elegant Card Case, suitable to keep them in when not in use, and then in handsome dozen boxes for the trade.

Two Sample Packs in Card Cases, sent, post-paid, on receipt of $1. Address
AMERICAN CARD COMPANY.
455 Broadway, or 165 William St., N. Y.

Patriotic playing cards advertised in *Harper's Weekly.*

railings were taken for fuel by soldiers when encamped there. He gave me a word of parting advice – not to speak of Rebels, 'an offensive word'. With this, we parted and I walked downhill in the pleasant and warm half moonlight.

I was anxious to know about General Thomas's answer if it had come. But, when I saw him, General Granger gave me no hope and handed me a pass back to Louisville. I went back to the hotel and then to the Sanitary Commission. Dr. Newberry said that if I waited for a day he would get me down to the front.

THURSDAY, NOVEMBER 19

Nashville

Here I am still on Thursday evening waiting for an early morning start tomorrow. Dr. Newberry described to me how he entered Nashville a year and a half ago with General Mitchell, finding great disorder there. He said he then realized for the first time how the contest was 'between autocracy and democracy'. The leading families had had things all their own way in Nashville.

This morning Dr. Newberry and Dr. Soule took me up with them to see the Sanitary Commission's soldiers' home – sixty beds and room for more. Dr. Newberry then took me to the Capitol Library. After that I went to have an interview with Governor Andrew Johnson the Military Governor of Tennessee, who had risen from being a shoemaker – a thickset, whiskerless man. Hence to a shop where I bought a knife and left my saddle bags to be mended.

SATURDAY, NOVEMBER 21

Bridgeport, Alabama

Joined Dr. Newberry and Dr. Soule yesterday, November 20th, at the Nashville depot at 7.30 a.m. Found them in a rail car crammed with officers and soldiers. Newberry got a seat by giving a dollar to a nigger servant of Colonel Anderson, with whom he had been last night. Colonel Anderson has been in charge of this railroad most of the War. He told Newberry some of the recent history. Not long ago Grant telegraphed that there was not a loaf in Chattanooga : now the supply has just drawn ahead of the demand. What saved the army was General Hooker's movement in Lookout Valley on October 28, which freed the river from Bridgeport up to Kelley's Ford. General Grant found two infirm little steamboats, had them tinkered up for service, and by means of them fed and saved the army. My informant was Colonel Hastings of the 33rd Mass. of the 11th Corps under Howard. The pontoon bridge here at Bridgeport has been constantly employed since Sunday by Sherman's army, now believed to be near Hooker or gone to Trenton, Georgia.

To return to our journey: we passed over the battlefields of Murfreesboro and Stones River and I made out the cedar brake and the desolation of the plain covered with blackened stumps with here and there a piece of a gun carriage or a bit of light blue greatcoat. Then we crossed Stones River and saw a considerable camp on the south side of it. I saw three ladies riding by the fortifications, the ladies riding as usual here without an extra skirt. Rain incessant and country broken. A long rise took us up to Tullahoma where we dined and then overtook a freight train and joined onto it. The freight waggons were covered with soldiers sitting on top of them in the rain. At Stevenson, Alabama, the train stopped and we got into a hospital car for the remaining ten miles to Bridgeport on the Tennessee River. The hospital car had twenty-four bunks hung on elastic springs. The doctor in command was going down to Bridgeport to collect a load of wounded. He gave us supper in a kitchen car next to the engine with very bad springs. A negro and two white cooks were round the stove and we stood balancing the coffee cups in our hands. The side of the car was open and we saw the rainy darkness and wooded hillsides of south Tennessee.

We got to Bridgeport about 8.00 p.m. in the evening (Friday, November 20), and slept comfortably in the Sanitary Commission's tent. Before I went to sleep I heard a solemn thudding sound outside. I asked my companion what was it and he said: 'Oh, the last of Sherman's men crossing the pontoons.' Bridgeport is the departure point for the new communications line which General Grant opened up to replace the long forty-mile track northwards across the mountains. This new line goes first by steamer from Bridgeport to Kelly's Ferry, then by waggon track across to Brown's Ferry where the river is crossed, from there the track goes over the neck of land which ends at Mocassin Point to cross the Tennessee river once again just north of Chattanooga.

A captain came into our tent to beg shelter. He had been very ill with kidney disease since the battle of Stones River and now wants to get to his unit at the front to arrange his discharge. Slept well in spite of pattering rain all night. The two boats which ply from here to Kelly's Ferry left yesterday. One of them may return this morning. The view from the tent is of the river looking south with cloud covered hills beyond it and the camp sloping down to the river. A lot of cavalry passed by in the rain. A negro stood at a table outside the tent in the wet cooking on a small wood fire.

It rained till afternoon. I walked with Col. Hastings to a hill close by with a battery on it, commanding the bridge which was being repaired. The river

The *Chattanooga*, in which Yates Thompson travelled up the Tennessee River
(from *Harper's Weekly*).

is 400 or 500 yards wide here with a long island opposite with tents on it. Dr.
Hastings gave me an account of his regiment attacking by night the ridge between
Lookout and Racoon Mountain close under Lookout. The ridge was very steep.
As they were marching past it, the Rebels had sent them a volley – so they
formed and charged up the hill. There was hand to hand fighting at the top, the
men using the butts of their rifles and shouting Gettysburg. The Rebels were
Longstreet's men.

We moved down to Chaplain Kennedy's tent near the river just above the
bridge. He is a stout person from Ohio and desired leave of absence having been
fifteen months out. He lived at the end of a long tent containing soldiers at
the other end. He was at Chickamauga and described how he became involved
in one of the Rebel attacks. I went out of the tent to look around and found
the steamer, *Chattanooga*, being loaded with hard tack in fifty-pound boxes,
ammunition (in boxes containing 1,000 rounds of ball cartridges), rifles in deal
boxes and forage (oats in sacks). The boxes were slid down the steep river bank

Signal post

← Chatanooga

ambulances in waiting to cross.

Taken near the ponton bridge
wh we were not allowed to cross on Sunday
afternoon Nov 22. 1863.

on plank runs, darkies standing round to steady them. Behind Kennedy's tent four darkies were singing: 'The Kingdom Coming'.

We went on board the *Chattanooga* at 5.00 p.m. and within an hour were in motion. Newberry and I sat on a pile of forage sacks making a bulwark on the lower deck. Next to me on the sacks was a soldier of the Potomac army going to join Hooker's troops.

I shall not forget that slow eight hours voyage to Kelly's Ferry. The rickety little steamer puffing and wheezing along, heaped up with as heavy a load as she could hope to take of biscuit, forage, and ammunition; we passengers dangling our legs from the sacks and boxes as we watched the moon and discussed the chances of being shot at from the shore. We munched army biscuit as we talked. The passengers were mostly hirsute soldiers in light blue greatcoats and capes. As we went along the clouds rose and the half moon appeared. We saw here and there the fires of camps and pickets and we passed a ridge of fringed hills about 1,200 feet high. We met the other boat at half-way.

Dr. Newberry discoursed to me about the Sanitary Commission and his

Lookout Mtn

Lookout Valley behind you her river

Sketch in Yates Thompson's small notebook of the bank of the Tennessee River on November 22 before crossing by ferry to Chattanooga (*see* page 147).

journeys in the Rocky Mountains when he was surgeon attached to exploring parties in Oregon, Colorado and New Mexico. The Sanitary Commission is divided into several Departments — the Department of Inspection employing surgeons to go round all camps and advise military surgeons and officers; the Soldiers' Homes Department for assisting men separated from their regiments; the Information Department for keeping lists of all men in hospital for the information of families and friends; and the Supply Department for distributing and filling up gaps in the supplies of the Army Commissary Department.

SUNDAY, NOVEMBER 22

Kelly's Ferry

We arrived at Kelly's Ferry after midnight (November 22) by moonlight.

[145]

Chattanooga from the north bank of the Tennessee River (from *Harper's Weekly*).

The boat took some time to get alongside. Finally we landed in the moonlight and walked to the Sanitary Commission tents where we were looked after by a Mr. Sutcliffe. Dr. Soule and I had a tent to ourselves with a wood fire and blankets. We talked of College and then slept well.

We woke this morning in a dense fog. When it cleared we saw a lovely landscape – the river winding between wooded rocky hills, the steamboat lying as we had left her and the hooped baggage waggons carrying away their cargo through the mud while empty waggons struggled up to the side of the boat. We fed well and started off on our journey at about 9 a.m. Mr. Sutcliffe introduced us to the colonel in charge, a tall light-bearded man who said polite things about the Sanitary Commission. So we set off on our walk to Chattanooga along General Grant's waggon track. This was a ten-mile walk with the road deep in mud and long strings of struggling waggons along it. Dead and dying mules and horses by the roadside showed the strain endured by this supply route. Our track led up a steep ascent and through a wooded defile which opened out onto an open space of corn and we had a good view of Lookout Mountain. We

[146]

stopped and watched the puffs of shells from the Rebel batteries on Lookout. A soldier asked me if I was a sutler. The road was crowded with waggons. We soon entered another sunken defile between wooded hills where several regiments were encamped. This was about the middle of the broken valley between Lookout and Racoon. We stopped and drank brandy sitting on a rotten tree trunk which lay across a brook in an open space among the trees, facing Lookout and the camps of the New York regiments, Hooker's men from the Army of the Potomac, on the ridge between us and Lookout. A German soldier came along and said they expected a battle and that he was sick of fighting. He was from a German regiment. Cavalry and infantry were moving through the wood on the march in the same direction as us; they were probably the detachment of Hooker's army which I saw afterwards march into Chattanooga. One line of infantry came past us on the track: they were at the easy and they chaffed at my saddlebags. We emerged at the river Tennessee at Brown's Ferry after crossing a ravine. The pontoon bridge was being repaired, having been opened to let pass some Rebel rafts sent down to break it. So we took the ferry and a U.S. officer with a lady embarked with us. Arrived on the other side we walked by a corduroy road two or three miles across the spit of land enclosed by the bend in the river which ends in Mocassin Point opposite Lookout Mountain. We came to the river again close by another bridge leading to Chattanooga. Here we were sent a mile up river to cross by ferry: we walked along the river bank and sat waiting for some twenty minutes by the landing stage for the ferry boat. There was a great crowd of men and horses waiting with us. The boat (or raft) swung Rhine fashion from the point just above us. I washed myself at the brink of the river — hands, face and feet — taking great pleasure in the scene in front of me. Finally we got across and found our way to the Sanitary Commission in the main street of Chattanooga running north and south.

We soon set out again to see the town, first south along the main street, then turning to the left (or east) we went through scattered houses and clustering tents to Fort Wood. Here we saw a line of spectators watching the flight of the shells fired from Fort Wood. We joined them on a ridge by Fort Wood facing Missionary Ridge and with my glass I saw Rebels in the valley on the outskirts of a wood. We saw some shells burst some way south just below Missionary Ridge. The sun set below Racoon Mountain. To the south beyond Lookout was a lower peak looking very picturesque. We could just distinguish the white house near the top of Lookout, 2,700 feet above the river.

As we came back to the town some five or six regiments marched past us

The illustration on the pages overleaf shows Chattanooga and the Federal encampment (from *Harper's Weekly*).

by fours at the shoulder arms, colours flying, music playing. They belonged to the 11th Corps and among them we saw Col. Hastings of the 33rd Massachusetts regiment on horseback. He recognized us and waved his hand at me. Some 2,000 men must have passed in full marching order, knapsacks and blankets on their backs, pans and pots swinging – Hooker's men from Lookout Valley. The Sanitary Commission people – and indeed all here – expect an immediate battle.

Had a good supper. After supper Dr. Soule and I went to the Christian Commission to sleep. There we met the Rev. Mr. Smith and a lot of other employees of the Christian Commission and also a correspondent of the *Cincinatti Gazette*, who was a consequential snob, and Mrs. Dickinson of the Sanitary Commission. Soule and I slept together. I slept well.

MONDAY, NOVEMBER 23

Chattanooga

Breakfasted on cornbread and bacon, with apple sauce and butter from Ohio and coffee at the Christian Commission. Went out with Newberry and Soule – north along the main street to the river where lay some rafts and the steamer *Dunbar* under repair. The *Dunbar* is to run the gauntlet of the Lookout batteries to Brown's Ferry to help supply the army. We went towards the bend of the river and I continued on alone to Fort Wood. I got there about midday. From there I had a fine view of the whole Rebel position on Missionary Ridge about three miles distant across a wooded valley. The pickets and the skirmishers of both sides were behind their respective rifle pits in the valley below us and the Rebel pickets were plainly visible from Fort Wood, about half a mile from where I stood. All those round me were expecting immediate fighting.

Soon I saw a sight I shall never forget. The whole Union army in the town – about 25,000 men under General Thomas – left their tents and huts and marched out past Fort Wood in long winding columns creeping into the valley and into line of battle round the town. From Fort Wood it all looked like a great review. But it was in deadly earnest. At about two o'clock the line of skirmishers began to advance and they crossed the open space in front of me in two lines : they had not gone far before the pop of rifles showed that they had come across the Rebel pickets. The whole army then advanced in two lines and plunged into the wood at the foot of Missionary Ridge. The musketry continued incessantly until dark. The great guns on Fort Wood, 32-pounder Parrotts, opened fire twenty yards from where I stood, throwing shells at the ridge opposite. Wounded men limped back up towards us and General Thomas stood watching close by me. Ambulances hurried forward for the badly hurt. The men cheered as they charged. Very soon a batch of about 200 Rebel prisoners were brought in — rough and ragged men with no vestige of a uniform, but with good shoes and looking well fed. One huge fellow with a great red beard and long hair to match, his face bloody from a ghastly wound on the forehead, brought up the rear, as they marched close by where General Grant and General Thomas stood on Fort Wood. There was a great galloping of aides de camp, a hurrying of waggons and ambulances, the scream of shells and the whistle of bullets.

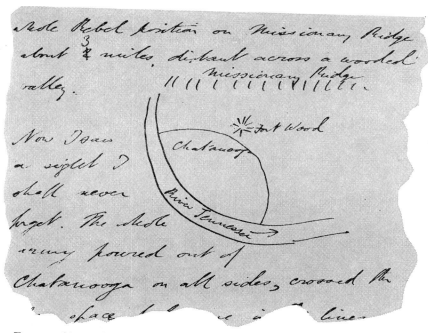

Extract of letter from Yates Thompson to his brother, Rodie, November 23, 1863.

The result of this afternoon's work is that the Rebel picket line, including a knoll called Orchard Knob, has been captured. General Thomas and his army are lying out on the ground tonight in the positions they have taken in the valley without tents and in the rain. Perhaps they will storm the Ridge tomorrow.

I have been busy tonight rolling bandages for a kind sister of mercy here: 131 men are in hospital in Chattanooga for wounds received today. I suppose there are more wounded who have not yet been fetched in. This is war with a vengeance.

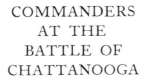
COMMANDERS
AT THE
BATTLE OF
CHATTANOOGA

**Maj.-Gen. Ulysses S. Grant
Commander of the Federal Armies
in the West.**

**General Braxton Bra
Commander of the Confederate Arm
in the We**

Maj.-Gen. William T. Sherman
(Federal Army of the Tennessee).

Maj.-Gen. Joseph Hooker
(detachment from the Federal
Army of the Potomac).

Maj.-Gen. George H. Th
(Federal Army of the Cumberl

*(All by courtesy of the
National Archives)*

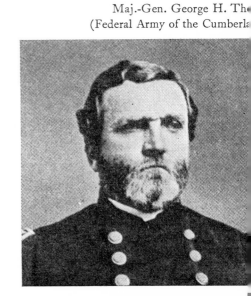

TUESDAY, NOVEMBER 24

Chattanooga

First thing after breakfast this morning I went to Fort Wood. General Thomas's men were still where we left them last night extending in a great semi-circle all the distance from the river above Chattanooga to the river below towards Lookout Mountain.

Shells were being fired from Fort Wood intermittently. I saw the Carl Schwarz division at the left by the river advance across three fields of wheat stubble – skirmishers in front, then a formation in line supporting the skirmishers and then a body of men in a square. The skirmishers halted at the edge of a cornfield and I saw no further advance made here before the rain obscured the view. General Howard's brigade is on the left of Schwarz. The Rebels in force were plainly visible, General Howard's at one point on the top of Missionary Ridge – tents and men quite discernible.

At ten o'clock we saw a number of pontoons floating slowly down the river. At first this puzzled the spectators at Fort Wood. But it was soon learned that these pontoons had formed a bridge by which General Sherman's army had crossed the Tennessee River upstream. He now had no further use for them and we knew he was safely across. I talked to a gunner of the Michigan Battery manning Fort Wood. He was a regular some time before the War. The guns are 32-pounder Parrotts: the shells have not been exploding too often.

After seeing the pontoons we knew that Sherman was across the Tennessee. We heard his artillery all through that day, but could not see much of what he was doing. We heard in the evening that he was established on the north end of Missionary Ridge. The mound (Orchard Knob) occupied yesterday had Unionist guns mounted upon it and fired occasionally.

I began to think nothing was doing when at about midday, when I was dividing my lunch with one of the gunners on the fort, heavy reports of cannon and musketry from Lookout Valley made all of us hurry to that side of Fort Wood. I joined two officers looking through telescopes towards Lookout Mountain and we soon saw Hooker attacking, his men plainly visible to us sweeping round the steep face of Lookout.

Close by me was General Grant in a black surtout with black braid on and quite loose, black trousers and a black wideawake hat and thin Wellington boots. He looked clean and gentlemanly but not military having a stoop and a full reddish beard, the moustache much lighter than the ends which were trained to a peak. General Hunter[4] was with him his black wideawake

4. General David Hunter, sent on a special mission by Stanton, Secretary of War, to report on Grant. After Chattanooga he told Stanton that he had been constantly with Grant (he slept in Grant's tent) and that he was both hard working and temperate – 'he only took two drinks during the three weeks I was with him'. Washington was keeping a watch on Grant through Generals Hunter and Meigs.

[153]

Extract from the Diary, November 24, describing General Grant at the
Battle of Chattanooga.

having gold cord round it but having the brim turned down all round over his cadaverous face. Quartermaster-General Meigs [Quartermaster-General of the U.S.] was also there with grey beard, a fine looking man of from 50 to 60.

We saw Hooker's men fall back once – then they advanced again. After some little suspense we saw the Rebels run round the face of Lookout near the top and Hooker's line advance after them, rifles popping all along the face of the mountain and guns shelling the retreating Rebels from Mocassin Point and Fort Negley. An officer beside me with a telescope cried out: 'There they are and the Rebels are running.' His glass was pointed to the steep face of Lookout more than half way up – and there sure enough, just three miles from us along the sparsely wooded face of the mountain, we saw a running fight with the Rebels retreating before Hooker's men.

General Grant watched it all from Fort Wood with General Hunter and Quartermaster-General Meigs. Grant wearing his plain wideawake such as I was wearing and with nothing military about him except a large opera glass.

Furious cheering soon started on the Federal right down in the plain near the river, where they could see the action better than we could from Fort Wood. Above the sound of the popping of the rifles and the roar of the artillery arose a great shout through the whole valley of Chattanooga. From Fort Wood we could see plainly with a glass the Union soldiers near the top of the mountain carrying a great Stars and Stripes flag. Now all down the valley right along to the extreme left, where Sherman's men could hardly have known what it was all about, rose the cheers of victory. The spectators in the town of Chattanooga took up the cry; and I never in my life saw anything like the excitement on Fort Wood. Of all I saw and heard today the most impressive circumstance was the cheering of the Union troops marshalled in line of battle in the positions to which they advanced yesterday and where they had passed a tentless night and had been standing idle all morning. When Hooker's men planted that large U.S. flag near the top of the mountain, the whole of the troops, and the people in and around Chattanooga, who must number some 60,000 at least, seemed to hurrah together.

The only man who seemed unmoved was General Grant himself, the prime author of all this hurly burly. There he stood in his plain citizen's clothes looking through his double field-glasses apparently totally unmoved. I stood within a few feet of him and I could hardly believe that here was this famous commander, the model, as it seemed to me, of a modest and homely but efficient Yankee general. I stood next to General Grant for quite some time. If the battle had been a pageant got up for my benefit I could not have had it better.

[155]

Entrenchment of Thomas's Corp (from *Battles and Leaders of the Civil War*).

Federal troops landing at Brown's Ferry (from *Battles and Leaders of the Civil War*).

Wartime view of Chattanooga (courtesy of the National Archives).

General Hooker's column storming Lookout Mountain (from *Harper's Weekly*).

Hooker telegraphed to General Grant saying he had 500 prisoners and all seemed to be going well when rain came on and nothing more was visible.

After we lost sight of Lookout Mountain and Hooker's attack grew more silent, I observed General Grant walk to the other side of the fort and order some shells to be thrown into the Rebel camp on Missionary Ridge. 'I guess that half a dozen will be enough', I heard him say.

It now came on to rain more heavily, coming from the south. Lookout Mountain and the rest of our view had disappeared. We heard the battle still raging in the clouds above but we saw no more that afternoon. I crouched under the parapet of the fort for some time next to General Hunter. H. S. Doggett of the *Cincinatti Times* was at the fort and he gave me half an onion and some bread to eat. Finally I went back to Chattanooga and found Dr. Soule who borrowed my cape to go out.

It is 9 p.m. as I write this. The weather has cleared up. The moon is near full and shining brightly. I have just been out at the back of our house where two sentinels are sitting over a wood fire guarding the adjacent hospital. They belong to the 124th Ohio regiment which was badly cut up in the fight I saw from Fort Wood yesterday. I left them and walked up to Signal Hill and from there I saw the whole panorama that I now knew so well with Lookout Mountain standing black against the sky. Musketry flashes continued incessantly all over the mountain and the Union camp fires were one continuous blaze. All along Missionary Ridge the Rebel army kept up a glaring line of camp fires which merged on the extreme left with the fires of Sherman's men.

So ended Tuesday, November 24, the second day of the battle. When I came in from my walk I heard that Sherman had taken the northern point of Missionary Ridge and that Hooker in the south had effected his junction with Thomas's right. Tomorrow morning either the Rebels will run or there will be a general attack on their whole line.

Confederate battery on top of Lookout Mountain (from *Harper's Weekly*).

TUESDAY, NOVEMBER 24

Letter to brother Rodie

It has been a wonderful chance to see war on so gigantic a scale under such pleasant circumstances. We feed capitally on the Sanitary Commission's stores and sleep under a roof every night. It must be seldom that battles can be seen like this.

Today a poor fellow walked up to Fort Wood and lay down and died in front of us. The deaths and wounds are horrible. I never see a wounded man without thinking how wicked politicians are to begin a war such as this.

The flashes from the pickets' rifles on Lookout tonight is very beautiful to see at

To the top of Lookout mountain
(from *Harper's Weekly*).

a distance; but close up one would see two lots of men chiefly of English descent dodging about among trunks of trees and rocks, one side in blue cloth and the other in butternut cloth but not in uniform, shooting one another whenever a chance offers like Red Indians, scarcely keeping their footing on the steep side of the mountain with those below in danger of rocks from those above. When a man is wounded he must limp or crawl like a rabbit among the rocks until picked up and put on a painful stretcher and carried with many jolts down the mountain to a still more painful ambulance, then perhaps to die of gangrene in one of the crowded hospitals of Chattanooga.

One sups full of horrors. Yet my coming here was a great piece of luck. My pass is in the name of J. A. Anderson of California, an agent of the Sanitary Commission,

The summit of Lookout
Mountain (from *Harper's
Weekly*).

who had to go back at Nashville. Dr. Newberry, chief of the Sanitary Commission in the West, took me along with him as Mr. Anderson. I hope no harm will come of it. There was no other possibility of getting here and there is I believe not a single civilian with the army except one or two newspaper correspondents. The only misfortune is that being under an alias I cannot present my letters, of which I have several, to officers here. Dr. N. very naturally does not want it to be generally known that he has smuggled me here. It is my opinion that tomorrow will see a very important episode of the War and that many more men on both sides will bite the dust.

WEDNESDAY, NOVEMBER 25
Chattanooga

I write this in an upper room of the Chattanooga Store of the U.S. Sanitary Commission. I went out again after breakfast to Fort Wood walking part way with an Ohio soldier who arrived late last night from Bridgeport, eager to join

Grant (bottom left), with his staff on Lookout Mountain on November 26 (courtesy The National Archives).

his regiment at the front. General Grant's headquarters today were advanced from Fort Wood to Orchard Knob where I did not have the temerity to follow him.

At Fort Wood I first looked towards Lookout; two telescopes lay side by side on a gun embrasure of red iron-stained soil and a bearded Federal was looking through one of them. I took the other and we made out a battery among trees on the top with dark clad soldiers loafing about the embrasures. The white house and its outbuildings, with a line of rifle pits sloping downwards from them,

Sunrise on Lookout Mountain, November 25 (from *Harper's Weekly*).

is occupied by Federals. Soon I saw a Federal on the top cliff waving a black and white signal flag. The Rebels quitted the top yesterday; and Dr. M. C. Read of the Sanitary Commission who went up on to Lookout this morning to look after Hooker's wounded found them nearly all provided for — he carried off a loaded rifle, marked Tower 1861, which lay by a dead Rebel.

A lieutenant came up near me and began signalling Fort Negley. I went to the eastern side of the fort and watched Missionary Ridge from there. The air was sharp and clear. The smoke of Sherman's camp fires was plainly visible and

[161]

his attack on the left continued all day. The firing of cannon and musketry was chiefly on our left and we could see Rebel troops hurrying along Missionary Ridge — here a mounted officer and there a battery, all plainly visible to the naked eye, moving to their right to repel General Sherman's assault. And one assault of his they did repel. There was a large cornfield on this part of the Ridge side. We watched with breathless interest a dark line of Unionists cross this field diagonally under heavy fire. We saw them disappear into a wood above the field and thought they had taken the battery. But no, they were only sheltering in the wood from the storm of shot and shell. For about an hour they stayed there. But then we saw them fall back in pell-mell confusion across the cornfield which they had crossed in such gallant style before.

After this there was a pause along the front. Then suddenly at 3 p.m. the whole Unionist line, which had lain so quiet yesterday in the valley, advanced against Missionary Ridge. Heavy firing flared up along the whole line and I saw three masses of Federals march out in front of their batteries. What a rare spectacle it was with the glassy and curving river behind us and on our right the plain of Lookout Valley with reserves and ambulances in the foreground, and galloping orderlies and stragglers and mule-drawn country waggons in the middle distance — the leafless woods opening here and there to show fields where sometimes I could plainly see skirmishers and lines of troops advancing to the thicker growth at the foot of the Ridge. The reserves followed a field or two behind in solid masses.

When the lines reached the foot of the Ridge they became half hid in the thick undergrowth. At about 3.30 p.m. heavy firing intensified and I saw three groups of Federals emerge and march up the steep slope. Each had three or four or five regimental flags which marked their progress to the naked eye. They were received with heavy fire — but on they went. We held our breath as we watched them. I believe they took about half an hour to scale the Ridge. It seemed two hours to me. We saw them all get to the top. I don't know who got to the top first of the parties that I could see from Fort Wood, but I thought it was Sheridan's.

Suddenly the Rebel batteries — and then all the batteries on both sides along the whole line, except a few in front of Sherman where some more shots were fired — became silent. We knew then that a great victory had been won. I returned at dark to Chattanooga.

Let me now describe my trip to the field of battle by moonlight. At eight o'clock news was brought to the Sanitary Commission that there were some wounded needing everything, in a house at the foot of the Ridge. Coffee, preserved milk, whisky, crackers, lemons, etc. were at once collected and put into an ambulance in which Dr. Newberry and Mrs. Dickinson rode. I crept over

[162]

the box seat into another ambulance sitting under the canvassed hoops on bags of cotton wool put there for the wounded. We jolted off at a brisk trot. Passing near Fort Wood on our right we went along a snake fenced lane through strips of timber and open fields and a hollow where were the huts of a Rebel encampment. We saw Union fires on top of the Ridge and some more fires lower down. Driving through a copse we at last saw several white roofs of ambulances outside a white wooden house.

The house had five windows at the front and a light wooden fence enclosed what had been the garden. Several ambulances were at the door. We hurried into the house carrying our supplies. On entering the parlour we saw to the right a low room with a colour print of Henry Clay over the chimney piece, papers scattered all over the floor, and three dead Unionists lying there. One of the dead men was a captain, and his face was streaked and clotted with blood he having been shot through the heart and having bled at the mouth. His arms were crossed.

One of the duties of the Sanitary Commission is to make out the names of the dead. We did this from letters in their pockets and pinned their names to their breasts. The first name to be found was John Bull — the first dead Yankee I saw was called John Bull. Having covered their faces, we could do no more for them.

Mrs. Dickinson set about cooking and we went out to look for the wounded. We went towards the top of the Ridge climbing over a breastwork of tree trunks. We talked to a soldier who was warming his feet at an old Rebel fire. He said we should go straight on up the hill where there might be more wounded; but he thought almost all had been brought in. We went up through felled and growing trees to the top of the Ridge where a soldier directed us to a log house where wounded men had been collected.

It was a two-roomed house with a log-supported loggia along the front, on which were laid the dead. In front of the house were laid some six or eight wounded men round a camp fire, some of them moaning. One of them, a captain, with a wound in his hip, sat on a chair by the fire. He told me how he was knocked down by a shell bursting near him and found he was wounded in his hip when he got up. Inside the house in the room on the right we found some fifteen desperately wounded men, more than half of them Rebels. We went the round of them giving them whisky and feeling their foreheads. We started one of them off on a stretcher down the steep hill. One Irishman expressed great surprise that we attended the Rebels. We then set off downhill. The Ridge was alive with fires. Those on our left were Thomas's corps. A white mist hung over the valley. We got back to the first house without incident. Nearby we found a man with a swollen and gory cheek, moaning and speechless. Mrs. Dickinson

[163]

washed and bandaged him and an ambulance took him away with the wounded man whom we had sent down from the top. We followed the ambulance walking. Along with us came a Rebel Captain Lawrence, of St. Louis, Missouri, who had come into the lines from Hardee's corps by way of the railroad. He was a middle-aged thickset man, with a peaked beard, moustache and whiskers shaved, in a dark jacket and pants and calf high boots, a satchel slung over his shoulder and a bundle in waterproof under one arm. He said that Bragg had 45,000 men and that Hardee's corps had captured 800 of Sherman's men. He thought the North was too strong for the South — but the South would never give in. He was glad to have a whole skin after nine pitched battles and would like to go home and 'never fight more'. He said he knew Chattanooga well — 'Some mighty fine girls there', whom he used to escort to a Baptist church which we passed.

Got back by full moonlight — 1.30 a.m. on November 26, night clear and cold. We then sent off stores to 300 of Sherman's wounded said to be in need of everything — and so to bed.

THURSDAY, NOVEMBER 26

1.40 p.m. I am sitting on a rock just beneath the top crag of Lookout Mountain. These crags are 60 to 100 feet high and there are cracks or gaps in them. A few minutes ago I mounted up one of these up a rope ladder of fifteen to twenty rungs. On getting to the top I heard a voice above saying: 'Friend you can't come here.' On telling him I wanted to get to the white house to look for wounded I was advised to return the way I came — 'Express orders from General Hooker.' The soldier was in a blue topcoat and I only saw half of him over the rock.

This is the west side of Lookout. I started climbing up from the junction of the Tennessee River and the Lookout Creek. On the road near the bottom I met a young fellow from Sherman's corps who had been left behind. We stood and listened and counted the guns fired from Fort Wood in honour of the victory — there should have been thirty-four but we made it thirty-five. I went on and was soon walking with a bearded man on a bay horse, coming from Rossville where Hooker stayed last night, after carrying the Ridge and flanking the Rebels. I went then up the steep hill through felled and standing timber till I came out at a breastwork guarded by two men with twenty fresh graves nearby with bits of hard tack box material at the head of each with the name, etcetera, of the dead man scrawled on the back in pencil. In the breastwork were hundreds of Rebel rifles marked Tower 1860. I went obliquely round the hill finding every good defensive place a breastwork or shelter. I climbed steeply again up a huge boulder and there I left my opera glasses!!

FRIDAY, NOVEMBER 27

Started out with Dr. Soule at 8.30 a.m. Went with him to the foot of Lookout and then on alone up Lookout Valley through Rebel camps strewn with deal boxes, tin utensils, etc. Foraging Federals were searching around.

Sketch of Grant and Sherman at the Battle of Chattanooga, the last battle they fought together (courtesy Edward Eberstadt and Sons from *The Civil War*, American Heritage).

I spoke with a man in butternut who was standing by the road. He showed me the Georgia boundary. He had left his house from fear of Federal shells from a Mocassin Point battery and now occupied a house of a Rebel who had gone south taking his slaves along with him. He told me that the white house belongs to a Mr. Craven, a rich man owning the fields between Chattanooga Creek and the Tennessee river — also gone south with his slaves. He said the Rebels used civilians worse than the Federals. Longstreet's men were near here before Bragg sent him off to East Tennessee. The Rebel camps that I had

[165]

passed were evacuated on Tuesday night. The trains went by all through the night: the Rebels much disheartened.

I then came to some farm buildings. There was a yellow flag up. A Federal officer was talking to a Confederate surgeon who was looking after eleven of Longstreet's men, who had been wounded in the fight of October 28. He told us Longstreet's men were far better disciplined than Bragg's. I went on through the wood to a few houses and saw an old woman washing butternut clothes in a tub and asked her for some water. She gave me some in a gourd, having no glass or cup. Late on Tuesday afternoon she saw two Rebels sitting on a rail and heard several shots go close by her.

I went on to the Chattanooga Creek, here clean and pretty rapid. I found a bridge and crossed into the main road from Chattanooga to Rossville and overtook three Federals going out to join Osterhaus's* division under Sherman's command. They had made the march from Corinth; but had been left behind. They said that wherever they had been they had seen Rebel deserters. I left them at the Rossville Gap and went to the top of Missionary Ridge. There were great signs of fighting along the top. The trees were spotted with bullets and I picked up several. I saw three or four dead Rebels lying as they had fallen. The first gave me a shock. I came on him quite suddenly, his butternut clothing being the same colour as the leaves he was lying on; his head and feet were bare: he had thick red hair and beard and his feet looked very white. He lay on his back with his shirt open and hole in his breast. There was little blood. The next man lay on his face, black hair, holes in his boots.

I came to where Sheridan's men had attacked through a hickory and oak wood. Here a sturdy Illinois soldier told me how he had come up. He fired five times as he came up the hill: 'You see that log beyond yonder torn hickory', he said, 'I was behind it when a shell hit the tree a foot above my head. I have it here,' and he showed me a disfigured bullet. They chased the Rebels down the other side of the Ridge and he and his friend captured a Rebel major. 'He was riding up,' said the soldier, 'and my friend took a level on him and told him to surrender: he wheeled his horse round to run so suddenly that it fell' – and my Federal took him.

One hundred yards on I found Bragg's headquarters, a farmhouse with outbuildings. Here was a pile of Rebel rifles picked up on the hillside, about 500 I guess.

I went on to a knoll commanding the ridge in both directions. Here had been an attack: there was a trench saturated with blood from dead Rebels lying there. I was near the small house where we came on Wednesday night. I found two Rebels – one dead and one just alive unattended since the battle. I gave the wounded man what brandy I had left in my flask and he spoke a little. His brains were protruding – the wound was in the back of his head. He seemed thankful for the brandy. I minced and mixed some meat, onions and biscuit and put water with them. He tried to eat but could not chew. A Federal came to help and washed his face and was most indignant with the Rebel doctor who cared only to get away instead of staying with the wounded. The wounded man said, 'Yes that's so.' He was a tall thin-faced fellow with black hair and dirty teeth.

A lieutenant came up to find out who I was. He walked with me to the field where I had seen Sherman's men repulsed. Here we met two children, a little girl and a boy who had collected several dozen bullets. The little girl said she lived 'over there', pointing to Bragg's headquarters. She had been in the house all through the battle. She never thought the Rebels would go. Her father was in the army at Mobile. Near us were three or four Rebel dead and one Federal. Others were scattered about everywhere.

We crossed the railroad passing over the short tunnel and up the hill attacked by Sherman. Many unused shells lying around, trees fearfully cut about. We passed six or seven graves. The lieutenant picked up a bullet with a bit of blue cloth stuck to it. The field was ploughed up with shot and shell. The lieutenant had a negro boy whom he called Nimbus. He made him carry water-proofs which he had picked up and bullets which he intended to make into a set of chess men.

I left him and hurried on because the sun was setting. Crossed a deep ravine and came to where the railroad passes into the open. Here was a line of rifle trenches taken, I suppose, on Monday. As I came into the town a number of cavalrymen were entering and I asked one of them the news. He was one of 1,500 men sent to Cleveland where they had burnt some factories, blown up a magazine and captured a lot of waggons. This morning they had been attacked by Buckner with artillery and got away after a fight – they knew nothing of the victory here.

I made the main street and by dodging got in without being asked the countersign though it was an hour after sundown. I must have walked twenty-four miles. I supped and got ready to go.

Dr. Newberry handed me this pass:

No. 220 Transportation Office,
Chattanooga, Tenn.

Pass for steamer for Bridgeport, Ala.
J. Anderson.

Nature of Service – Sanitary Commission
H. H. Johnson
Capt. A.Q.M.

November 27, 1863.

[167]

Missed the steamer *Dunbar* which had left earlier for Kelly's Ferry. Saw fires in the distance which I took to be Cleveland. Now I am tired to death.

SATURDAY, NOVEMBER 28

Kelly's Ferry, 11 P.M.

Am by myself in a snug tent with a fire in the stone chimney and milk punch warming by it in a coffee pot, and my pants drying on a stool.

I set off this morning with Dr. Soule and two lieutenants and several men who had come to Chattanooga as escorts for some deserters and were returning to join their regiment which guards the Nashville–Bridgeport railroad. We tramped along the tracks. I stopped in a cave under Lookout to put on my cape and missed the others. So I pushed on alone. I got lost at Hooker's Ridge and asked my way at a house. A well-spoken man directed me. He showed me where Hooker began his assault of Lookout. I went on past waggons stuck in the mud, in the darkness through deep slime till I got to Mr. Sutcliffe's tent at Kelly's Ferry. The rest have not yet come.

Had a good supper with Sutcliffe – beef tea, corn beef, beans, preserved currants, biscuits, tea, fresh butter, etc. The walk was as tiring a thing as I have done yet. It was hard to keep on the muddy track and I reeled about often in the dark. What has happened to poor Dr. Soule? The *Dunbar* is lying here and goes back to Chattanooga tomorrow.

WEDNESDAY, DECEMBER 2

Nashville, Tennessee

I must describe my three days' journey from Kelly's Ferry to Nashville.

On Sunday, November 29, I got up at daybreak in my snug tent where a darkie had already made a fire. I was just dressed when in came Dr. Soule, Lieutenant Spruce of Waterbury, Conn., and the other lieutenant from Connecticut, both of whom had started with us from Chattanooga. They had lain out one and a half miles from the ferry by the roadside and had had a miserable night. I gave them the remains of my milk punch and we soon got breakfast. A band of prisoners, said to number 3,500, now made their appearance having marched all night from Chattanooga. They had a guard of about 150 men but they could have easily escaped had they cared to. They looked picturesque on the hillside above us. I watched them get their rations – a ragged cap was filled with biscuits and a good joint of meat added. Most of those I saw looked over-joyed at what they got and some said 'bully' in unmistakable accents. One Irishman turned with a hearty laugh to the Federals watching and said, 'Oh you God-damned rebels, you!'. There was much rough good humour on both sides. All the prisoners had canteens and blankets – the blanket being often a quilt or a piece of carpet. All had shoes.

With warm adieus to Mr. Sutcliffe we departed in the *Chattanooga* to Bridgeport – a cold ride down the Tennessee. Talked about sport with Lieutenant Spruce and danced to keep my feet warm with a Rebel prisoner. The prisoner was an Irishman from Limerick and Nashville who had enlisted before secession, made prisoner at Donelson and twice besides – but taken back on parole and so obliged to go on fighting. The banks of the river are wooded and often steep and rocky and very beautiful at many of the curves of the river. Everywhere the mistletoe abounds, cedar and holly with red berries and great stems of vines. Strings of ducks of various kinds fly past and a few rifles are fired at them from the bows of one of the barges on tow.

At Bridgeport I sat in the tent of the Sanitary Commission and told my story till supper came. Supper was followed by drowsy talk. A tall black-bearded Yankee in charge of transportation told us of the terrible difficulty of the supply route to Chattanooga before the river was opened to Kelly's Ferry. On Monday, November 30, at 2 p.m. we were woken and hurried to the freight car from our contiguous beds.

In the freight car we found a green wood fire which almost stifled us and a crowd of some twenty people. We spent about two hours in the car, an old major amusing me much by his good-humoured endurance. He said he had lost one eye through the smoke but could last on the other. We stopped about half a mile from Stevenson and got out to walk. Dr. Soule was much alarmed by the apparent height of the jump from the car to the frost bound earth. We found a brightly burning wood fire by the track and lay down by it. There was no wind and by spreading my blankets I got warm and comfortable and fell asleep. Awakened at crack of dawn and invited to a church occupied by the Christian Commission on the hill above Stevenson among cedars. Here cots were fixed round a spacious room with cracks between the logs and a small stove. I crawled into one of the cots and knew nothing till I was awakened to breakfast in full daylight – coffee, boiled ham, etc. seemed like the food of the gods.

There was no train to Nashville owing to an accident. So at midday we visited the two lieutenants. They lived in a roomy frame and tent edifice with a stove. They received us cordially and asked us to dinner. Soule declined though I would have liked to have stayed. I set out for a walk alone. Crossed a valley through a cornfield or two up to a cluster of cabins. Entered one and asked for

[169]

water. I sat with a man in butternut and three girls. He said he was a Union man as were all in that valley. He had a small basket of cotton in the house and showed me where it was gathered — a patch of small bushes with a dead horse nearby. They spun their own cloth ; but had no dye except walnut.

I got to Stevenson and saw a squad of darkies in a double line, their names being called over. A black sergeant told me they were on their way to the front. Some of them were quite light coloured. They were in great good humour.

On Tuesday, December 1, we were up at dawn and got seats in a stoveless car to Tullahoma. Here we waited twenty minutes for dinner. Soule and I examined a stockade such as scores we had seen along the track.

Finally we got to Nashville. On arrival there I went to see Dr. Lindsley and told my story. Mrs. Lindsley wanted to make out that no Federal advantage had been gained by the battle!

WEDNESDAY, DECEMBER 2
Munfordville, Kentucky

This morning in Nashville : up at 5.30 a.m. Talked to the landlord. He is a Union man but in favour of slavery as 'divine and natural'. We got to the railcars by omnibus at 7 a.m. I put my valise into the baggage car and was getting into the passenger car when I was stopped — no citizens to get in until all soldiers were placed. Dr. Soule was equally aghast with me. Happily I got into the baggage car, Dr. Soule being, I think, left behind. I got seated on my valise and saddle bags next to two soldiers belonging to the Twelfth army corps. They were in Geary's brigade and had left Chattanooga on Friday by the boat we had missed. I read *Red Gauntlet* and talked to the soldiers till we stopped at Glasgow junction where we waited for the Louisville train to pass. I bought for three dollars some Confederate money from some of the prisoners of whom there were three cars full on the train.

At Munfordville there was an ambulance but no other carriage to convey us to the town. It had come to meet the General in command of southern Kentucky, Hobson by name. I made bold to ask him to carry my valise up to town, half a mile : he responded by carrying myself up too. The hotel entrance was through a grocery store of a low order. An officer came in with me to recommend me to the landlord. Immediately he left there issued from under the counter a scrubby soldier whom I imagined to be a deserter.

I went out to call on Colonel Thomas Wood. He came out to my knock and greeted me kindly. He leaves tomorrow for Frankfort to attend the Legislature and is full of business. He will give me an hour if I come to tea at six.

[170]

He looked taller than ever and a trifle harassed and anxious, I thought. He told me he was the father of General Wood, whose brigade I saw charge up Missionary Ridge and after whom Fort Wood was named. He introduced me to his daughter, Mrs. Coombs, and I left to come again at six. Went for a walk. Crossed a pontoon bridge over the Green River. On the south side I found a guardhouse with four soldiers and a sergeant who demanded my pass. Had none. Could they not pass me? Could not. The lieutenant was coming and would punish them. Said I would wait for the lieutenant and sat down to warm myself at their fire. Soon up came the lieutenant: he said, 'quite against rules'. I asked him to make an exception to prove the rule — one of the most impudent things I ever said. He consented and I walked beside his horse up the hill and on to an earthwork where there were a lot of graves. He said this had been the Rebel position during the battle. I looked over the river and saw a regiment on parade.

Back to town and to Colonel Wood. He met me at the open door and took me into the parlour where we fell to talking. Soon we had supper where were Mrs. Crompton, Colonel Locke of Franklin, going tomorrow to Louisville, and Mrs. Coombs. Venison steaks from a young buck killed near the Mammoth Cave and as tender as possible. We talked of slavery. Colonel Wood holds it no sin to own a slave. They are 'an inferior race' and he has a horror of their being put on an equality with the whites. He would like to have the State clear of negroes. They are 'revengeful, indolent, incapable, etc.' But he agreed with me that they looked thriving in Hamilton, Ontario. Colonel Locke said there was much running away of slaves in Kentucky. Colonel Wood has been a magistrate for forty-three years. Years ago a case was brought to him of a free negro wanting a licence to marry a free negress. He granted it and has done so ever since. But many magistrates in Kentucky refuse and hold that a free negro should take up with a woman as a slave does without a licensed marriage. Colonel Locke said that Colonel Wood had taken the common sense view, but he thought the law was on the other side.

THURSDAY, DECEMBER 3

Colonel Wood came in at 10.30 a.m. when I had just finished writing my journal. Taking me out with him into the street he introduced me Mr. R. P. Munford, son of the founder of the settlement in 1800 A.D. Went with him to Colonel Locke's headquarters. Found he was out. Mr. Munford gave me a long account of a wound received by him in the shoulder and arm. He had

[171]

possession of some rebel secrets told him in confidence by a Rebel colonel, who commanded the Rebel forces south of the river. He told a ruffian he could have Munford's farm if he put him out of the way. The ruffian shot at Munford, who was probably the first man wounded in Kentucky. I went with him to the Provost Marshal's office and got my pass renewed by a lieutenant. Then got a boy to carry my things to the rail car and just caught the train. Met a captain of scouts who range along the Nashville/Bridgeport railroad in plain clothes. He has lost twenty-two men out of his company, five of whom were hanged. His company has now taken more than 500 prisoners. He likes scouting better than anything else notwithstanding the danger.

Got to the Cave City Hotel kept by a Major Owsley of the Kentucky Cavalry.

FRIDAY, DECEMBER 4

Mammoth Cave

Into the Mammoth Cave after breakfast with my friend Captain Reid (of the scouts), Lieutenant Gwynne and three soldiers, led by Mat, a mulatto anxious to please us. The cave opening is 300 yards from the hotel.

In the afternoon sat in the hotel with 'my crowd'. They played cards and went out now and then to have a drink at the bar. They were a strange group. A long-shanked Kentuckian major with black beard and moustache looked on at the card game rolling a cigar in his mouth, two corporals, and myself reading at the fire's edge.

I wished I was in Louisville. The journey will be tedious and may be dangerous. The stay here is menaced by those cut-throat guerillas and there is always doubt about the arrival of the train from Nashville.

MONDAY, DECEMBER 7

Burnett House, Cincinatti, Ohio

Arrived here this evening travel stained after three days getting here from Mammoth Cave – dull days compared with my unforgettable days at Chattanooga; but such as they are I will chronicle them.

I woke up at the Cave City Hotel on December 5, with a confused sound of heavy rain, footsteps along the corridors, loud talking and laughter. I went to sleep again and it was still raining when I came down to breakfast. I talked with two mulattos, John, the butler and Mat, our guide at the Caves. Mat said the slaves were running away fast. He pointed out a hulking darky who had been carried south by his owner, but had got back through the Federal lines. Soon after breakfast our party packed into a carriage. I sat opposite Captain Reid of the Scouts and learnt much from him. He comes from New Hampshire and knows well my friends the Whites. He was at Dartmouth College when the War started and enlisted as a private in the Army of the Potomac. His service of 'scouting' is organized and is known as 'guerilla-ing'. He and his men wore plain clothes: otherwise they would be shot from the first cover. Several of his men have been hanged. They receive extra pay from the Secret Service Bureau. Captain Reid told me how he had once been taken prisoner and lay with his captors in a log house at Lebanon, Tennessee. They were all asleep when the old woman of the house shook him awake and told him to be off. He went; and once fifty yards from the house he was safe in the rough country.

The morning was hazy and the blue misty air hung in the valleys in the sun in between the wooded hills. We got to the railroad in plenty of time. I got a snug seat in the Ladies' car to Louisville with a large window opening on the country at the back of the train.

Arrived at Louisville. In the omnibus from the depot was a man from the front. He said he had seen several heads of Yankees stuck on stakes and un-buried bodies lying in the road, waggons driving over them. After tea I found my way to the Sanitary Commission. Just outside the gates where I met my first rebel prisoner, three weeks ago, I met Dr. Newberry. I went in and found Soule. There was much talk about an expected collision between the Sanitary Commission and the Christian Commission. On Sunday, December 6, I had an interesting talk with Dr. Newberry. He seems really to like me. He thinks of educating his children in Germany and this might bring him to England.

I left at noon by river in the steamboat *Major Anderson*. On the boat I talked with a German captain in the Ordnance Department — an exile from Hesse Cassel since 1849. He despises this country. 'No discipline in the army, low-bred women, no chance for a foreigner in the army.' He is a disappointed man; he used to be friendly with Sigel* and Osterhaus, but they have shot above him now. He lives at Dayton, Ohio.

At supper I sat next to a man who asked the waiter to cut his meat and I saw that he had no right arm. He had been wounded at Chickamauga and lay out nine days in the field.

Landed at Cincinatti at daybreak today, December 7. Wrote to papa, Dr. Newberry, and Dr. Soule.

WEDNESDAY, DECEMBER 9

New York

The dreaded long journey from Bridgeport is ended. I left Cincinatti at 6.00 a.m. yesterday, dinner at Alliance, clean sleeping car, woke at Harrisburg this morning, missed the connection at Philadelphia, called on Dr. Furness and left him a letter not finding him in, lost my ticket but brazened it out, crossed the Hudson river by steamboat to New York and so by street car along Broadway and Sixth Avenue to the Brevoort House. Letters from mother. Meggie, Mr. White of Keene and Mr. May of Syracuse awaiting me. Things to get tomorrow – photographs of Cambridge, Mass., for Henry Bright, sewing machines for Mrs. Hale and Mrs. White.

And so to bed. How lucky I have been on this journey since I left New York on September 18 until today December 9.

Is my luck to hold till I get back to Liverpool?

THURSDAY, DECEMBER 10

New York

Went from Wall Street by ferry to Brooklyn and walked to 64 Pierpoint Street to visit Dr. Storrs the notable divine whom I met in July in the White Mountains. Mrs. Storrs is a niece of Wendell Philips. I found the family at home and they kept me for tea. Dr. Storrs met Mr. Everett last night at the Brevoort. Mr. E. is sanguine about a change of feeling in the South; he thinks Lee's generalship questionable at Gettysburg; and the special honours now talked of for Grant a neglect of Meade. Miss Storrs met William Everett at tea and says he was very dirty and talked a great deal about his recent visit to Gettysburg.

FRIDAY, DECEMBER 11

New York

I spent the evening at Mr. Brevoort's house three miles from Brooklyn. Mr. Brevoort is a little man with brown whiskers and moustache and a pleasant manner. He showed me an original portrait of Washington by Pine in 1785 without the false teeth of the later portraits – also a letter of General Washington speaking jocosely of sitting for portraits and a little book with a diary of

Washington on a visit to New York beginning, 'exercised in my carriage at one o'clock' – also a beautiful missal with seventy-four miniatures picked up by Mr. Brevoorts' father in Paris. At supper we had canvas-back duck and sixty-year old madeira in demijohns whose wickerwork had rotted with age.

SATURDAY, DECEMBER 12

New York

Did little today. Found Greeley again away and shall give him up now. Called on Mr. Irvin at his office. He is to be married on Thursday.

SUNDAY, DECEMBER 13

New York

I got to Dr. Storrs' church in Brooklyn (Pilgrim's Church) when he was in the middle of his sermon. I had missed the ferry. Dr. Storrs was preaching a thanksgiving sermon in connection with the President's letter about the success in East Tennessee. The Storrs took me home to dinner with them. I like them very much. In the afternoon I went to hear Dr. Beecher* preach. It was the best sermon I ever heard – not only the best sermon but more entertaining than any comedy.

Tomorrow I am off to visit the Whites at Keene for two days and thence to Boston for a week before sailing home in the *Canada* on December 23 across the grey and melancholy waste.

*   *   *

Editor's Postscript

So end the Yates Thompson diaries of 1863.

The letter from the Rev. W. O. White awaiting him in New York had invited him to visit Keene once more before leaving for home. 'There can be no picnic parties,' added Mrs. White, 'but we will keep you warm and snug and love you too if that agrees with you.'

My great-uncle was twenty-five on December 15, 1863, and he could hardly have found a more congenial place in which to enjoy his birthday than under the hospitable roof of the Rev. W. O. White of Keene, New Hampshire, who remained his friend for more than forty years thereafter.

Henry Yates Thompson, aged 88.

Biographical Notes

ANDERSON, Major Robert. Surrendered Fort Sumter, off Charleston, South Carolina, after it was bombarded by Confederate artillery on April 12, 1861. This signalled the official beginning of the Civil War.

BEAUREGARD, Pierre Gustave. Confederate General commanding the batteries which opened fire on Fort Sumter on April 12, 1861.

BEECHER, Henry Ward (1813–87). Brother of Harriet Beecher Stowe; a staunch abolitionist and an influential public man; his sermons at Plymouth Church, Brooklyn, were famous.

BRAGG, Braxton (1817–76). Confederate General; in June 1863 he was appointed to the command of the Confederate 'Armies in the West'; defeated Rosecrans at Chickamauga in September 1863; retreated into Georgia after his defeat by Grant at Chattanooga in November and relieved of his command in December 1863.

BRECKINRIDGE, John Cabell (1821–75). Extreme pro-slavery Democrat from Kentucky; accepted nomination for the presidency in 1860 from a breakaway group of Southern cotton states and split the Democratic vote. He became one of the more successful 'political generals' of the War and ended as Confederate Secretary of War. At Chattanooga he commanded a division on Missionary Ridge.

BRIGHT, John (1811–89). English statesman and parliamentarian; a strong supporter of the North.

BROWN, John (1800–59). Fanatical opponent of slavery; attempted to raise an insurrection of slaves in 1859 at Harper's Ferry in Virginia; he was captured by a detachment of U.S. Marines under the command of Robert E. Lee; he was tried and hanged.

BUELL, Don Carlos, Unionist General. Commanded the Unionist Army of the Cumberland until replaced by Rosecrans towards the end of 1862.

BURNSIDE, Ambrose E. (1824–81) Unionist General. Appointed by Lincoln to command the Army of the Potomac, November 7, 1862 in place of General McClellan; on his appointment he said, 'I am not competent to command such a large army'; he was proved to be right. Burnside is better known to history for the growth of hair on his cheeks, named after him as 'sideburns', than for his generalship.

BUTLER, Benjamin F. (1818–93) Unionist General. A Breckinridge Democrat from Massachusetts, he was loyal to the Union when Secession came. For political reasons he was given a number of high commands in the Unionist armies, but he proved to be a bad general.

CALHOUN, John Caldwell (1772–1850). A politician who carried immense influence in the South and a prime mover of Secession. Vice-President in 1828 under President Andrew Jackson.

CHASE, Samuel E. (1808–73). Senator from Ohio; like Seward a candidate for the Republican presidential nomination in 1860; Secretary of the Treasury in Lincoln's cabinet; aspired to the presidential nomination again in 1864; a strong abolitionist.

CHILD, Francis James (1825–96). Boylston Professor of Philosophy and Rhetoric at Harvard.

COLFAX, Schuyler (1823–25). Speaker of the House of Representatives; Vice-President in Grant's first term, 1869–72.

COBDEN, Richard (1804–65). English statesman; with his friend, John Bright, founded the Anti-Corn Law League; both were staunch supporters of the Northern cause.

DANA, Richard Henry (1815–82). Federal District Attorney for Massachusetts; assumed a place in American literature as author of *Two Years Before the Mast*; appointed by Grant, when President, as Minister to London but the Senate refused to confirm him; Yates Thompson heard him speak at a gathering of Harvard alumni in July 1863.

DAVIS, Jefferson (1808–89). President of the Confederate States of America, February 1861 to April 1865; captured by Unionist cavalry in May 1865; a state prisoner for two years at Fortress Monroe; released on bond, May 1867.

DOUGLAS, Stephen A. (1813–63). A powerful political figure, he was elected to the Senate in 1847. Lincoln fought him in 1856 and 1858 in the contest for the Illinois senatorship, thereby becoming a national figure. In the 1860 election Douglas was the official Democratic candidate and polled a large popular vote. Lincoln won largely because the Democratic vote was split by the supporters of Breckinridge. When Fort Sumter fell Douglas pledged his support to Lincoln in defence of the Union.

EMERSON, Ralph Waldo (1803–82). Poet. 'Few Americans have been more picturesque; none holds a solider place in the history of American life' (*Dictionary of American Biography*). Yates Thompson met him with Hawthorne at Concord, Mass.

FISHER, George Park (1827–1909). Professor of Divinity at Yale.

FURNESS, Dr. William (1802–96). Unitarian clergyman; life-long friend of Ralph Waldo Emerson; became pastor of the Unitarian Church in Philadelphia; a noted preacher, scholar and abolitionist.

GAMBLE, Hamilton R. (1798–1864). Governor of Missouri; he kept the state loyal to the Union.

GARRISON, William Lloyd (1805–72). Fanatical abolishionist; founded the newspaper 'The Liberator' in 1831 in Boston and fought an unrelenting campaign against slavery until 1865.

GRANT, General Ulysses S. (1822–85). Appointed the only Lieutenant-General in the Federal army and General-in-Chief of all the armies of the United States in March 1864; President of the United States, 1869–77.

GREELEY, Horace (1811–72). A strong abolitionist and intensively active editor of *The New York Tribune*. As Democratic presidential candidate in 1872, he unsuccessfully opposed Grant's election for a second term. America's 'greatest editor, perhaps it's greatest popular educator and certainly one of it's greatest moral leaders' (*Dictionary of American Biography*).

HALE, Edward Everett (1822–1909). Nephew of Edward Everett; Unitarian clergyman; author of *The Man Without a Country*.

HALLECK, H. W. (1815–72) Unionist General. Held command in the western theatre until he was transferred to Washington in July 1862, where he was in overall charge of the campaigns of all the Federal armies under the direct supervision of Lincoln and Stanton. On Grant's promotion in March 1864 to Lieutenant-General and General-in-Chief of the armies, Halleck, who remained a Major-General, was outranked by him as were all the other general officers in the Federal armies. Thenceforth until the end of the War his position was that of Chief-of-Staff.

HILL, Dr. Thomas. President of Harvard, 1862–68; Unitarian clergyman and scientist.

HOLMES, Oliver Wendell (1809–94). Poet, essayist and physician; author of *The Autocrat of the Breakfast Table*. Yates Thompson met him dining with Edward Everett in Boston.

HOOKER, Joseph (1814–79). Unionist General; succeeded Burnside in command of the Army of the Potomac in March 1863 but was defeated at Chancellorsville in May. At the Battle of Chattanooga he organized the successful assault on Lookout Mountain.

JACKSON, Thomas Jonathan (Stonewall) (1824–63). Confederate General. Lee's ablest lieutenant; his death at Chancellorsville in May 1863 at the moment of victory was a severe blow to the Confederate cause.

JOHNSON, Andrew (1808–75). Military Governor of Tennessee; Vice-President in 1864 when Lincoln was elected for a second term and became President of the United States when Lincoln was assassinated on April 15, 1865.

JOHNSTON, Joseph E. (1807–91) Confederate General. In December 1863, after Bragg's defeat at Chattanooga, he was placed in command of the Confederate 'Armies in the West'; he surrendered to Sherman in April 1865.

JOHNSTONE, Albert Sydney, Confederate General. Commanded the Confederate armies in the western theatre until killed at Shiloh (or Pittsburg Landing) in April 1862.

LEE, Robert E. (1807–70). In May 1862 took command of the Confederate Army of Northern Virginia; proved himself a master of strategy and a great and colourful leader of men. Until Grant became General-in-Chief of the Federal armies in 1864 Lee generally won battles against the Army of the Potomac although with fewer men and inferior equipment; surrendered what was left of his army to Grant at Appomattox Court House on April 9, 1865.

LINDSLEY, John Berrien (1822–97). He became Chancellor of the University of Nashville in 1855. He was in charge of the Confederate Military Hospitals in Nashville until the Unionists occupied the town after Fort Donelson fell in February 1862. A Presbyterian clergyman, he was widely respected for his single-minded devotion to the cause of public health.

LOWELL, James Russell (1819–91). Poet, editor, critic. Yates Thompson met him at Harvard on Commencement Day in July 1863. At that time he was very hostile to England, but at a much later date he was a successful American Minister to London.

McCLELLAN, George Brinton (1826–85) Unionist General. The hope of the Unionists, he was appointed by Lincoln to the command of the Army of the Potomac in July 1861. He was a good organizer but as a field commander turned out to be a failure and he was ruined by vanity. Lincoln dismissed him in October 1862 and he was never again employed on active service. In the 1864 election, having been adopted as its presidential candidate by the Democratic party, he was soundly defeated by Lincoln.

MASON, James Murray (1798–1871). Known to history for the *Trent* affair; Senator from Virginia; the British Government never received him officially when he was a Confederate Commissioner in Europe.

MAY, Samuel Joseph (1797–1871). Secretary to the Massachusetts Anti-Slavery Society and a well-known abolitionist.

MEADE, George (1815–72). Unionist General who replaced Hooker in command of the Army of the Potomac on the eve of the Battle of Gettysburg; was the fifth general to hold this command, in which he remained until the end of the War, although under the direction of Grant in the field after March 1864 when Grant was made General-in-Chief of the Unionist armies.

MORGAN, John. A dashing Confederate cavalry leader who rode into Kentucky with 900 troopers in July 1862 and did much damage.

NORTON, Charles Eliot (1827–1908). Distinguished man of letters; friend of Ruskin and the Brownings; Professor of History of the Fine Arts at Harvard.

OSTERHAUS, Peter J. A German commander who served under Sherman; was assigned to Hooker in Lookout Valley at the Battle of Chattanooga.

QUINCY, Josiah. President of Harvard 1829–45; former congressman and Mayor of Boston.

ROSECRANS, William S. (1819–98). Unionist General. Removed by Grant from command of the Army of the Cumberland after his defeat at the Battle of Chickamauga in September 1863.

SCHOULER, William (1814–72). Born in Scotland; newspaper editor and historian; Adjutant General of Massachusetts 1860–66 and in that office prevented a repetition of the New York Draft riots in Boston in July 1863.

SEWARD, William H. (1801–72). Lincoln's rival for the Republican leadership in 1860 and his Secretary of State during the Civil War; a strong man and an attractive figure.

SHERIDAN, Philip Henry (1831–88). An aggressive Unionist General and one of Grant's favourites.

SHERMAN, William Tecumseh (1820–91). Unionist general. Grant turned over to Sherman his command of the armies in the western theatre when he himself went east in March 1864 as commander of all the Federal armies. Famous for 'his march through Georgia': he accepted the surrender of General Joseph Johnston with the last surviving Confederate army in the field in April 1865.

SIBLEY, John Langton. Librarian of Harvard, 1856–77.

SIGEL, Franz. Promoted General in the Unionist armies for political reasons. He had emigrated to America from the Grand Duchy of Baden having participated in the 1848 revolution: had considerable influence over the German settlers in and around St. Louis, Missouri, whom he encouraged to enlist in the Unionist forces. He was a bad general and Grant relieved him of his command early in 1864.

SILLIMAN, Benjamin (1779–1864). A national figure; founder of *The American Journal of Science and the Arts*, one of the world's great scientific publications.

SILSBEE, Nathaniel. Treasurer of Harvard, 1862–76.

STANTON, Edwin M. (1814–69). Secretary of War in Lincoln's cabinet; able, energetic and patriotic.

STEPHEN, Sir Leslie (1832–1904). Later the editor of the *Dictionary of National Biography* which was founded by George Smith, Yates Thompson's father-in-law.

STOWE, Calvin Ellis (1802–86). The husband of Harriet Beecher Stowe. He was Professor of Sacred Literature at the Theological Seminary, Andover, Massachusetts.

STOWE, Harriet Elizabeth Beecher (1811–96). Published *Uncle Tom's Cabin* in 1852.

SUMNER, Senator Charles (1811–74). Elected Senator from Massachusetts in 1851. Chairman of the Senate Foreign Relations Committee during the Civil War, he played an important part in the conduct of foreign policy; a strong abolitionist and a man of great distinction.

THOMAS, George Henry (1816–70). Unionist General. Grant, in his 'Personal Memoirs', says that Thomas's dispositions were always good and that he could not be driven from a point he was given to hold. He commanded the Unionist Army of the Cumberland at the Battle of Chattanooga.

TREVELYAN, Professor George Macaulay (1876–1962). Son of Sir George Otto Trevelyan. Regius Professor of Modern History at Cambridge and Master of Trinity College.

TREVELYAN, Sir George Otto (1838–1928). Historian, man of letters and statesman; Yates Thompson's life-long friend from Harrow School and Trinity College Cambridge, until the year 1928 when they both died. Trevelyan wrote a six volume history of the American Revolution – of this work his son, Professor G. M. Trevelyan, wrote in *The Dictionary of National Biography*: 'it was not generally popular in England and part of the public regarded his point of view as too favourable to the Americans. But in America it did much to help the movement for reconciliation to England by exposing many anti-English myths and by emphasizing the strong element of opposition to the policy of George III.'

VALLANDIGHAM, Clement L. Democratic Congressman from Ohio; was opposed to the War and became a rallying point for the 'copperheads' in the North; was deported for uttering 'treasonable' speeches, but returned from Canada to Ohio unmolested to contest the election for State Governor in October 1863, in which he was soundly defeated.

WALKER, Dr. James. President of Harvard, 1853–60.

WARE, William (1797–1852). A Unitarian clergyman and popular writer of historical romances; *Zenobia or the Fall of Palmyra* was highly successful in England and America.

WINTHROP, Robert Charles (1809–94). Congressman and Senator for Massachusetts. President of the Masachusetts Historical Society for thirty years.

Index